THE WIND

IN MY SAILS

Sue Schaefer

THE WIND IN MY SAILS

Copyright 2021 - Sue Schaefer

All rights reserved.

DEDICATION

This book is dedicated to my sister Ruth
because she asked for it and I love her.
sue 2021

ACKNOWLEDGEMENTS

This is perhaps the most difficult part of this book for me to write because I don't have a plan for it. There are so many people I've written 'because of.' There are also those I've written 'in spite of.' To each of them I owe a debt of gratitude.

My sister has 'hinted' for years that she'd like a book of the 'thoughts.' She may have nagged a few times too. I wouldn't have done it without that and I love her so I really had no choice. "Thank you Ruth, ever so much."

Thanks to those dear friends of mine who through the years have been an inspiration to me, who have stuck with reading the 'thoughts' year after year, thought after thought. Your faithfulness has been always-noted and ever-appreciated.

Of course thank you to each of the sons, daughters-in-law and grandchildren along with my husband who have so often shown themselves to be stalwart companions both in life and here in print. Each one of you has brought light in my darkness.

Thank you, dear Dotty Schmitt and Junie Volk for your responses to my request to write a foreword. You both know me and have been tenacious, faithful companions, friends and life-blood to me. You are ever-present in my heart.

Thanks ever so much to Grammarly! Whoever thought this software up, needs to get an award! It's also a good place to lay blame if the grammar is incorrect.

Thanks to Scottslm from Pixabay for the cover. Exactly what I wanted and saw in my mind's eye. You rock!

Finally and forever, thanks be to God through Jesus Christ. You, by Your Holy Spirit, 'get me' and I love you. sue

"He makes the winds His messengers,

Flaming fire His ministers."

Psalm 104:4

TABLE OF CONTENTS

January

February

March

April

May

June

July

August

September

October

November

December

FOREWORD # 1

I walked into the small building that we had recently purchased for our church gatherings in northern Minnesota, and there she was, on her knees scrubbing the floor. I stood and looked at her and said, "Well Hello, and who are you?" She turned around, looked at me, and said "Well who are you"? and thus began a friendship that would last now for almost 50 years. Sue became one of my most faithful friends. She lived in our apartment house, was my husband's secretary, helped administrate our beloved Camp Dominion and became a treasured friend who has been and is absolutely dependable in any circumstance.

One of my favorite memories of Sue occurred soon after I'd given birth to our youngest daughter and was utterly exhausted because our precious Jenny had stayed awake much of the night. Sue came upstairs and took one look at me and said "You look awful. Give me that kid and get back to bed."

I've had many such encounters over the years with Sue and her unique way of sharing what she was thinking. I watched her mature in the things of the Lord and walked with her through her romance with her future husband Ulrich Schaefer. In fact, my husband Charles and I had the privilege of officiating at their marriage at Camp Dominion. I also observed her giving birth to five exceptional boys. I would often smile as I heard her interaction with them, firm, loving, and often quite funny. Her husband and she took many 'extras' into their home over the years. She also became quite a unique and sought-after educator. I remember many times of laughter and tears that we shared. Through it all Sue became one of the most faithful friends I've ever had and it is from this rich and varied background that she began to write daily devotionals. In fact, they are the first thing I look for as I check my email each morning. I have found that the

Scriptures and her accompanying 'thoughts' have been relevant and inspirational. It is with great delight that I write these words to highly recommend this daily devotional penned by my friend. The thoughts and Scriptures she has shared have come out of her walk with the Lord now these many years.

May you be inspired and encouraged to deepen your own relationship with the LOVER of your soul, our Lord Jesus Christ. It was a blessed day when our paths first crossed in the early 1970s dear Sue, and to you who are reading these precious devotionals, you too will discover a friend not only in Sue but primarily with the lover of your soul, our Lord Jesus. Enjoy and continue to grow in the grace and knowledge of the Lord. Thank you Sue for sharing your heart and your thoughts as always with honesty and transparency!

- Dotty Schmitt

wife of 57 years

mother of 3

grandmother of 5

pastor-teacher and lover of God

FOREWORD # 2

When Sue asked me to write the foreword for her new literary offering, "The Wind In My Sails," I was humbled and honored. Sue is one unique lady who I trust you will come to love as you get to know her through this devotional.

"The Wind In My Sails" is a compilation of Scripture verses with thoughts that Sue has emailed Monday through Friday to family and friends for years; I'm among those who receive them. It is one thing to write a devotional book and quite another to live a life of thoughtful devotion to the Lord, to His Word, and to your family; Sue lives such a life. She, with her husband, Ulrich, and their five married sons with their wives, and sixteen grandchildren live lives of devotion to Jesus, to each other, and to all who know them... The Schaefer family exemplifies the culture of the Kingdom to a world in desperate need of their King.

Sue's love of God's Word comes through her thought to begin each day. Her unique approach expressing the verse gives 'food for thought'---to ponder, to internalize, and to be transformed by the Lord through His Word.

This past September 28th of 2020, Sue sent the following verse and thought which endeared us to each other in a very special way—forever:

"Trust in the Lord forever, For in God the LORD, we have an everlasting Rock."

Isaiah 26:4

"The dictionary defines 'forever' as: without ever ending; eternally.

That's a LONG time! I believe this Word that I should trust God and that it is forever. He forever is an everlasting Rock. I'm betting my life on it and that's a pretty big deal for me. You too!

Happy Monday!"

All I could think of after reading this devotional thought was a song from an old movie—Breakfast at Tiffany's—starring Audrey Hepburn; the name of the song is Moon River. I wrote the lyrics in an email to Sue explaining how the words to the song wouldn't leave my thoughts. Her response: "Do you know Junie, that is one of my most favorite songs!"

Moon River - wider than a mile
I'm crossing you in style someday
Oh, dream maker
You heart breaker
Where ever you're going I'm going your way
Two drifters off to see the world
There's such a lot of world to see
We're after the same rainbow's end
Waiting round the bend
My Huckleberry friend,
Moon River and me

I'm looking forward to crossing Moon River in style someday; there Sue will be my Huckleberry friend—forever! When reading "The Wind In My Sails" perhaps Sue's thoughts will bring you to the same rainbow's end, and her everlasting Rock will become your everlasting Rock! Sue will then become your Huckleberry Friend--forever! Happy Reading!

June Volk
Authoress, Itinerant Teacher
Shellyandjunevolk.com

INTRODUCTION

For the past thirty-some years, as a way to keep me in the Scriptures, I've been sending out a 'thought' each weekday. For many of those years, it consisted of a Scripture only. There were a few days/weeks missed when moving to a new state or traveling but for the most part, every day, thought after thought.

A few years ago I began adding my own commentary, that is, what God was speaking to me in the moment usually during the wee hours of the morning as I read the Word, seeking to hear His voice.

At times this has come easily and at times I've felt that I've had to really struggle to hear Him. I haven't always wanted to pay attention nor to share for that matter, specific Scriptures which as you'll see, I've made mention of. Nevertheless, I've done it, always knowing that the Word stands on its own. It does not come back empty.

The list of folks receiving the 'thought' has varied. Some have gotten it from the beginning and some for a brief time. Many have dropped me a line themselves in response. I've always loved that...the Word in action. Every now and again I've asked those who wish to continue, to let me know. If I didn't hear back, they've been deleted with absolutely no hard feelings.

To share with any/all readers is a change for me. May God's Word bring life to you dear reader because in the end, that's truly all that matters. If you'd like to receive my 'thoughts' each weekday, drop me a line and I'll put you on my 'list.' Thanks!
sue

thoughts.sue.schaefer@gmail.com

January

January 01

Therefore, prepare your minds for action, keep sober *in spirit*, fix your hope completely on the grace to be brought to you at the revelation of Jesus Christ. As obedient children, do not be conformed to the former lusts *which were yours* in your ignorance, but like the Holy One who called you, be holy yourselves also in all *your* behavior; because it is written, "You shall be holy, for I am holy."

1 Peter 1:13-16

I typically associate 'lust' with sexual desire but here methinks it goes deeper. I've had a discussion with one of my sons about the difference between 'want' and 'need'. He's wiser than I am. Sometimes those 'wants' or dare I call them 'lusts', are so deeply ingrained, they become needs in one's soul. Never good. We are called to walk the walk of holiness. It is a walk where truly, the only thing we need is Jesus Christ.

January 02

He again fixes a certain day, "Today," saying through David
after so long a time just as has been said before,

"Today if you hear His voice,

Do not harden your hearts."

Hebrews 4:7

Yesterday I read something someone had written on social
media and let me tell you, I was aggravated and annoyed. I
thought I was justified in my self-righteous attitude and had
pretty much put on an armor of irritation and indignation
which I felt duty-bound to display, thank you very much. I
even thought about finding a Scripture to match my mood,
using it in the 'thought' for today. God showed me mercy
though and pointed me in another direction.

He has never hardened His heart toward me. He constantly
hears me and you know, He still speaks to me 'today.' He still
today, shows me compassion and today, shows me His
faithfulness. Let me never harden my heart toward Him and
because of Him, toward others and I am speaking on your
behalf when I ask the same thing for you.

January 03

"Come to Me, all who are weary and heavy-laden, and I will give you rest. Take My yoke upon you and learn from Me, for I am gentle and humble in heart, and you will find rest for your souls. For My yoke is easy and My burden is light."

Matthew 11:28-30

On the one side, salvation is free for the asking. On the other side, it cost me my life. I remember walking the streets of Grand Rapids, MN just a few days after accepting Jesus into my heart more or less on a dare (to Jesus Himself!), which He most graciously accepted BTW. In anguish, I cried out.

"Get me away from these crazy people!" I wanted Him but I wasn't at all sure about the rest of it! He did give me rest though and you know, His yoke hasn't chaffed me nor caused me to stumble under the load. I'm ever so grateful He didn't listen to me! Those 'crazy people' have been added to by the Giver and are a gift given to me in response to my cry. Those 'gifts' have lasted for the entirety of the rest of my life. Their name is 'friendship' and they too have lightened the load. A 'bonus' if you will. My life has been such a small price to pay. Same goes for you I'm pretty sure.

January 04

"With the kind

You show Yourself kind,

With the blameless

You show Yourself blameless;

With the pure

You show Yourself pure,

And with the perverted

You show Yourself astute.

"For You are my lamp, O Lord;

And the Lord illumines my darkness.

2 Samuel 22:26-27, 29

The world describes this as; "What goes around, comes around." It is a lie. God does not throw back at us what we regurgitate up, that which is sin. Instead, He lights the way for us to shine from within as we allow Him to come, to live with us.

Yesterday I received an email concerning someone I've been praying for, for years. It was good news and an absolute answer to prayer! The kindness of those around that person kept him, opened him up to the love of Jesus Christ. I'm so grateful to God and to those dear ones around him! They truly were and are a reflection of Jesus' life within them.

January 05

Therefore many other signs Jesus also performed in the presence of the disciples, which are not written in this book; but these have been written so that you may believe that Jesus is the Christ, the Son of God; and that believing you may have life in His name.

John 20:30-31

This is the "empty tomb" chapter, one of my favorites. For me, it is the summation of the entire Bible. "Believe" is the action word! It didn't take seeing the nail imprints on his hands nor putting my hand in His side for me to recognize Him as the Lord of my life but almost. He's performed 'other' signs that have made me believe.

I was never accused by God for my unbelief. I was simply made to believe.

January 06

Many are saying of my soul,

"There is no deliverance for him in God." *Selah.*

But You, O Lord, are a shield about me,

My glory, and the One who lifts my head.

Psalm 3:2-3

Most mornings I 'remind' God of His shield of protection roundabout my family and many of you, on my "thought" list. Countless are the weapons given us from Him and He as our "shield" is a defense, a strong defensive weapon to be sure. He declares through David that He is not only a "shield," He is also "my glory" and He is most assuredly "the One who lifts my head."

Isn't it grand that TODAY is every day in His kingdom? I experience His shield of protection and His glory roundabout TODAY! So do you! I just want to make sure He knows that I remember.

January 07

For You have been my help, And in the shadow of Your wings I sing for joy.

My soul clings to You; Your right hand upholds me.

Psalm 63:7-8

Here are some definitions of "upholds"

To support or defend, as against opposition or criticism

To keep up or keep from sinking; support

To lift upward; raise

I sing in the car. I just do. Have pretty much since I accepted Christ in my life. Whether I'm in a good mood, bad mood, or an indifferent mood, I still sing and when I do, almost always it is to God. It allows me to see from a different perspective. My eyes are opened to be able to identify the help He's given me or at least offered! I haven't always taken that help but it's been there. It is one of the ways I've learned to cling to Him and you know, He DOES uphold me. I sing when I'm not in the car too. Try it!

January 08

But you are a CHOSEN RACE, a royal PRIESTHOOD, A HOLY NATION, A PEOPLE for *God's* OWN POSSESSION so that you may proclaim the excellencies of Him who has called you out of darkness into His marvelous light; for you once were NOT A PEOPLE, but now you are THE PEOPLE OF GOD; you had NOT RECEIVED MERCY, but now you have RECEIVED MERCY.

1 Peter 2:9-10

So I'm not feeling like a "chosen people" or a "royal priesthood" and most certainly not like God's "special possession". .....and yet.....HE says I am! HE says I was called out of darkness into His light to declare HIS praises! I was once not a people but NOW, aha!!! I am a "people of God"! You are a PEOPLE too and most specifically, HIS people! WE as HIS people, no longer get to go by what we feel. We get to go by what we KNOW! We have received His mercy and because of that, we are CHOSEN, ROYAL, AND GOD'S SPECIAL POSSESSIONS. Can you imagine! Take up your crown folks, and put it on your head! Don't leave it laying on the ground!

January 09

The Lord is my shepherd, I shall not want.
He makes me lie down in green pastures;
He leads me beside quiet waters.
He restores my soul;
He guides me in the paths of righteousness
For His name's sake.

Psalm 23:1-3

Let me break it down for you...in exactly this order....

I SHALL NOT WANT

He MAKES me lie down

He LEADS me

He RESTORES me

He GUIDES me

Yesterday morning around 4:30 as I was working, I realized that I was tensing up. I mean REALLY tensing up. I kept trying to relax only to realize a few seconds later that I was back in stiff mode. What does this have to do with today's 'thought'? Well, it's about restoring. Interesting choice of words. It means to bring back into existence, to bring back to a state of soundness. I like that. He brings back my soul into a state of soundness. He literally brings it back into existence from having been lost. He doesn't stop there though. I don't get to stand still on the path. That's when I get into stiff mode. As only He can, He guides me in the paths of righteousness because of Who He Is! Will I find myself in the same state again? Probably. Will I remember this Scripture? Absolutely.

January 10

Let the peace of Christ rule in your hearts, to which indeed you were called in one body; and be thankful. Let the word of Christ richly dwell within you, with all wisdom teaching and admonishing one another with psalms *and* hymns *and* spiritual songs, singing with thankfulness in your hearts to God. Whatever you do in word or deed, *do* all in the name of the Lord Jesus, giving thanks through Him to God the Father.

Colossians 3:15-17

On the way to work this morning, I was 'fretting'...I was 'fretting' about the people I was praying for, I was 'fretting' about a direction for our families in the next years, I was just 'fretting.' In other words, I was walking and praying in the flesh. I know better! HE IS ALIVE AND HE IS ENOUGH! What He gives me is ENOUGH! Where He takes me is WHERE I NEED TO GO! When I put my loved ones (both family and dear friends) in His hands, where else could they be that is more secure? Peace doesn't get along well with worry nor fear. Sometimes I make the decision first and His peace comes and sometimes His peace comes first and then I make the decision. Both work.

January 11

And Jesus cried out and said, "He who believes in Me, does not believe in Me but in Him who sent Me. He who sees Me sees the One who sent Me. I have come *as* Light into the world, so that everyone who believes in Me will not remain in darkness.

John 12:44-46

One could write a book just about the book of John. The above 'thought' is though for me, the culmination, the end-all. I muddle around so often in the dark of my own imaginings. It requires a simple turning, a 'yes' to walk in the belief that He IS the Light of the world and I need never walk in darkness. You either.

January 12

He does not delight in the strength of the horse; He does not take pleasure in the legs of a man.

The Lord favors those who fear Him, Those who wait for His lovingkindness.

Psalm 147:10-11

I don't intentionally use specific 'thoughts in any sort of rotation or pre-planned order. Each morning I prayerfully consider what to use as I read the Word. The above Scripture is one of the ones that seem to come up at roughly the same time each year. I need to hear it! The following comment is from the last time I posted it.

Ugghh. Here it is again - the waiting. God knows it is just hard for me. It has produced endurance though which has enabled me to stand in the storm and an assurance that yes, He does favor those that wait for His goodness, His mercy, His justice to manifest itself in this lifetime and on His timeline! The strength of a horse and the legs of a man wears out. God doesn't.

January 13

Now He who supplies seed to the sower and bread for food will supply and multiply your seed for sowing and increase the harvest of your righteousness; you will be enriched in everything for all liberality, which through us is producing thanksgiving to God.

2 Corinthians 9:10 -11

Thanks be to God!

He gives seed to sow and bread to eat. There is food to eat while we are waiting for the growing part. I love this provision! It is hard to wait when one is hungry! The expectation here is that we sow what He provides, and it is that which increases the harvest of righteousness. When I can get beyond 'myself' and sow into those around me and into what God has asked me to put my hand to, the promise is that my harvest will increase so that I may give of it yet more generously. Yep, it does produce thanksgiving to God.

January 14

The Spirit and the bride say, "Come." And let the one who hears say, "Come." And let the one who is thirsty come; let the one who wishes take the water of life without cost.

Revelation 22:17

This is an invitation. There is available to me a water which fills me with life, and it is without cost. It is what quenches my soul's desire to be refreshed and to partake of life in Jesus Christ. It is what I turn to when I'm tired and weary and I've had enough. It is where I drink when I am boxed and tied up and can't seem to get myself out of the mess I'm in. It is where I go when I'm desperately worried about a loved one or someone whom God has put on my heart to pray for. It is for me, life-giving and whether I am desperate or afraid or simply in need of peace, it is that drink which saves me, always quenching the thirst of my soul. You too.

January 15

He pours contempt upon princes

And makes them wander in a pathless waste.

But He sets the needy securely on high away from affliction,

And makes *his* families like a flock.

The upright see it and are glad;

But all unrighteousness shuts its mouth.

Who is wise? Let him give heed to these things,

And consider the lovingkindnesses of the Lord.

Psalm 107:40-43

Sue's translation:

He keeps us tucked away in a place inaccessible to those people/things that would harm us and makes us into one family, not many families but rather ONE flock.

We His people see this and are glad in heart, ...because all unrighteousness shuts it's mouth in the face of Him who is All in All!

16

January 16

Therefore, let us fear if, while a promise remains of entering His rest, any one of you may seem to have come short of it. For indeed we have had good news preached to us, just as they also; but the word they heard did not profit them, because it was not united by faith in those who heard. For we who have believed enter that rest, just as He has said,

"As I swore in My wrath,

They shall not enter My rest,"

although His works were finished from the foundation of the world.

Hebrews 4:1-3

I had many people for many years, preach to me. I wouldn't have it. It pains me now to remember how incredibly mean and hurtful I was to the various ones, ridiculing them, swearing at them....you get the picture. One time though, a guy came along who was bold enough to say to me, "You will have to pay for everything you've ever done or you can allow someone else to pay."

I'd like to tell you the fear of the Lord right then, drove me into His arms. It took a bit more prodding but it was the beginning and it truly was both about the fear of God and about allowing Him to bring me to a place of rest in Him. I've been grateful for it pretty much, ever since!

January 17

For if you forgive others for their transgressions, your heavenly Father will also forgive you. But if you do not forgive others, then your Father will not forgive your transgressions.

Matthew 6:14-15

I will admit it. I don't particularly care for this Scripture. It uncomfortably puts the pressure on ME and truth to be told, it needs to too! Ughh. The cleansing of oneself is often uncomfortable, at least the deep scrubbing bits. Surface washing is easy.

Plain and simple....really.

January 18

"Pray, then, in this way
'Our Father who is in heaven,
Hallowed be Your name.
'Your kingdom come.
Your will be done,
On earth as it is in heaven.
'Give us this day our daily bread.'
And forgive us our debts, as we also have
forgiven our debtors.
'And do not lead us into temptation,
but deliver us from evil.
For Yours is the kingdom and the power and
the glory forever. Amen.'

Matthew 6:9-13

"Your will be done."

When I can't/don't know what to pray, there is this. It is a safe prayer for me in the midst of confusion. There is more though. God doesn't leave me with "Your will be done."

He gives, I take. He takes (me), I give. Same goes for you.

I'm grateful that every kingdom, every power and all glory are His. AMEN!

January 19

But what does it say? "The word is near you, in your mouth and in your heart"—that is, the word of faith which we are preaching, that if you confess with your mouth Jesus *as* Lord, and believe in your heart that God raised Him from the dead, you will be saved; for with the heart a person believes, resulting in righteousness, and with the mouth he confesses, resulting in salvation. For the Scripture says, "Whoever believes in Him will not be disappointed."

Romans 10:8-11

"There's a seat on the bus for you." I heard the pastor from King's Chapel in Fairfax VA speak these words as he ended his message. That is it exactly. Jesus Christ has made sure that I have a seat on the bus. I don't care where on the bus it is. If you aren't on the bus, climb aboard. The fare has been paid already. I'm just grateful to be there and I'm ever so grateful that I can expect to see you there too.

January 20

I am the door; if anyone enters through Me, he will be saved, and will go in and out and find pasture. The thief comes only to steal and kill and destroy; I came that they may have life, and have *it* abundantly.

John 10:9-10

I would like to say, 'in these days' but truthfully, it's 'every day' that it is ever more important to know the voice of the Shepard and trust Him to take me where I need to go.

I've thought a lot about this 'pasture' over the years. I will admit that at times I've simply grown tired of the grass which was offered. I've told Jesus that too because you know, He can hear it and understand what I'm saying. Not tired of Him, just tired of the particular pasture where I find myself. I've had worse pastures by far than the one I'm in today and of course, there are those times I've escorted myself off the cliff and He's had to come get me. The bottom line is, I'm saved and there will forever be pasture and it will be a nourishment to my body and to my soul and it will be the best pasture for me at the time. Same goes for you. Maybe someday mine will be beside the ocean. ;)

January 21

I will sing of the lovingkindness of the Lord forever;

To all generations I will make known Your faithfulness with my mouth.

For I have said, "Lovingkindness will be built up forever;

In the heavens You will establish Your faithfulness."

O Lord God of hosts, who is like You, O mighty Lord?

Your faithfulness also surrounds You.

Psalm 89:1-2, 8

Here then, is the answer to every question I may have and it is a commission I've been given to do! It is a message I must sing from the rooftops! I WILL SING OF THE LOVINGKINDNESS OF THE LORD FOREVER; TO ALL GENERATIONS, I WILL MAKE KNOWN YOUR FAITHFULNESS WITH MY MOUTH.

It makes no difference whether I'm on a mountain top, in my car or my house, or yes, even this book. I MUST MAKE KNOWN TO THE GENERATIONS TO COME, THAT HE IS EVER FAITHFUL! So must you.

January 22

Do you see a man who is hasty in his words?

There is more hope for a fool than for him.

A man's pride will bring him low,

But a humble spirit will obtain honor.

Proverbs 29:20, 23

One may be optimistic regarding a fool, believing that there will come a day, most likely like those around me saw me.... when as a young adult, I was both hasty AND a fool, truly believing I knew everything there was to know about negotiating/staggering through my life.

Hasty words know no boundaries and may be heard from anyone, in any walk of life. Pride has a lot to do with haste. When the two are combined, so often the result is sin spilling out one's mouth. Humility has the opposite effect. Its result brings so much more than honor. It carries with it healing, encouragement, and yes, faith and it's also contagious. So is haste I guess, in a truly nasty way.

January 23

"You have loved righteousness and hated lawlessness; Therefore God, Your God, has anointed You

With the oil of gladness above Your companions."

Hebrews 1:9

I initially wanted to put the parable of the ten virgins from Matthew 25 as the 'thought' for today. That led me to the above verse in Hebrews.

The culmination for us as believers is to see Jesus return to reign on the earth. We then, as per Matthew 25, must have always with us, the means to keep our lamps burning in preparation for His return! I believe the oil for our lamps is that very thing mentioned here in Hebrews, "the OIL OF GLADNESS"! This is what He makes available for us and His supply never runs out.

January 24

Let the one who does wrong, still do wrong; and the one who is filthy, still be filthy; and let the one who is righteous, still practice righteousness; and the one who is holy, still keep himself holy."

"Behold, I am coming quickly, and My reward *is* with Me, to render to every man according to what he has done. I am the Alpha and the Omega, the first and the last, the beginning and the end."

Revelation 22:11-13

I admit it. There have been times when the thought of Jesus returning in the midst of what I've purposed to do, has kept me from the doing of it.

I am reminded once again of the ten virgins in Matthew 25 who keep themselves ever ready, ever awaiting with anticipation, the return of the Bridegroom. We are called as the people of God to keep ourselves "still holy"! The virgins used the lampstands not only as a means to show their readiness, they also used them as a way to bring light. Light does away with filth. It beckons those nearby to come too.

January 25

Your people will volunteer freely in the day of Your power;

In holy array, from the womb of the dawn,

Your youth are to You *as* the dew.

Psalm 110:3

The literal translation of this is:

"Your people will be freewill offerings in the day of your army.

In the splendor of holiness, in the womb of the dawn,

The dew of your youth is yours."

I'm in THAT crowd! So are YOU!

January 26

Blessed *be* the God and Father of our Lord Jesus Christ, the Father of mercies and God of all comfort, who comforts us in all our affliction so that we will be able to comfort those who are in any affliction with the comfort with which we ourselves are comforted by God.

2 Corinthians 1:3-4

This is new for me. I don't often (almost never) look at an affliction as a means for me to be able to comfort someone else. I look at it as either God wanting to get my attention or satan trying to get my focus off of what God wants me to do.

.....so, the Father of ALL mercies, the God of ALL comfort, comforts me in ALL my affliction so that I am able to comfort those who are in ANY affliction with exactly the SAME comfort which I have been comforted! This isn't something I would choose for myself but I understand it, the more so in the many years I worked with kids but truly in so many situations. He has been ever faithful to me and kept me, always for His purposes, always. You too.

January 27

For all things *are* for your sakes, so that the grace which is spreading to more and more people may cause the giving of thanks to abound to the glory of God.

2 Corinthians 4:15

In our house and both in my husband's and my own prayer life, we almost always start out with, "Thank You for today." There is a recognition of His grace in our lives to give each of us what is needed, what must be recognized as coming from Him. Every glory, every honor is due Him. It is for us to make recognition, to proclaim the gift of grace He's given us.

"Thank You for today Lord Jesus. Thank you for the person reading this too."

January 28

Let the words of my mouth and the meditation of my heart be acceptable in Your sight,

O Lord, my rock and my Redeemer.

Psalm 19:14

On two occasions recently I heard different little bodies (a couple of the grandsons) use the word 'nasty.' I can guarantee you they heard it from me. It's my 'go to' word when I experience something I don't like or more probably in their case, when I see or have to clean up something 'nasty.' Now nasty isn't a bad word really but it isn't edifying either. While in the shower this evening it dawned on me that it's just not a word I need to use. My heart truly is to 'let the words of my mouth and the meditation of my heart' be pleasing in His sight. God's provision and the work He gives me to do isn't nasty. It is good and strengthening. Same goes for you, I'm pretty sure.

January 29

"Listen to me, you who pursue righteousness,

Who seek the Lord:

Look to the rock from which you were hewn

And to the quarry from which you were dug.

"Pay attention to Me, O My people,

And give ear to·Me, O My nation;

For a law will go forth from Me,

And I will set My justice for a light of the peoples.

Isaiah 51:1, 4

I have often envied the way my husband was brought up. I don't mean the 'God' part which portrays me as it should....more shallow than I care to admit. I mean the 'life part' where he was allowed to be just a boy, with seemingly no worries. Here is where I need to pay close attention to the Word. His law goes forth to everyone, in every situation. It brings justice with it and that justice lights the path for each individual 'people.' That's me and it's you. It is the reason that today and every day, we as a people must pursue righteousness, seek the Lord. I was hewn from the Rock that is Him and to disparage it is to scorn Him. It has been a life-long lesson for me to learn. He's helping me work it out.

January 30

Dead flies make a perfumer's oil stink, so a little foolishness is weightier than wisdom *and* honor. A wise man's heart *directs him* toward the right, but the foolish man's heart *directs him* toward the left.

Ecclesiastes 10:1-2

I know about dead flies. They are disgusting and in very short order, they dry out and when crushed, turn into yucky, useless dust. Foolishness is like that. When it settles, it spreads a black film of emptiness that leaves me feeling shallow and a buffoon. It literally takes a force of will at times for me to move toward what is honorable, what spreads life, and what is good. I don't always choose that way but you know, my ever-present companion, Jesus, is helping me. He's the best tutor in this school of life He has me attending. You too?

January 31

Say to the righteous that *it will go* well *with them*,

For they will eat the fruit of their actions.

Woe to the wicked! *It will go* badly *with him*,

For what he deserves will be done to him.

Isaiah 3:10-11

I was recently going to do something in anger. In the midst of doing it the Holy Spirit spoke to me, giving me the distinct impression that if I did this thing, there would be something broken, which it would be difficult to mend. Hmmm. Notice there's no "if" in the Word that says, "...it will go well with them, *for* they will eat the fruit of their actions. I believe it's all about learning to walk in righteousness. This is a living Word!

february

February 01

In John 21, Jesus gives Peter four words of instruction:

"Tend My lambs."

"Shepherd My sheep."

"Tend My sheep."

"Follow Me!"

Peter, turning around, *saw the disciple whom Jesus loved following *them*; the one who also had leaned back on His bosom at the supper and said, "Lord, who is the one who betrays You?" So Peter seeing him said to Jesus, "Lord, and what about this man?"

John 21:20-21

Peter had just been given some of the most talked-about tasks in history and what does he do? What an opportunity to pick Jesus' brain about how to go about the 'great commission!' Instead he chooses to 'deflect' in child behavior terms. Deflect means: Get your eyes off of me and on to someone else, usually used either because someone doesn't want to do what they've been told to do or because they're jealous of what someone else has or is doing.

May we be a people who don't 'deflect' but rather, do what He's instructed us to do, when He tells us to do it.

February 02

Light arises in the darkness for the upright;

He is gracious and compassionate and righteous.

He will not fear evil tidings;

His heart is steadfast, trusting in the Lord.

Psalm 112:4, 7

I used to 'do' drugs. After I was saved, I was baptized and believed that when I'd come out of the water, I'd been cleaned of all the residual drugs in my body. Flash forward a year or so. I was sitting in the kitchen of our church on a stool working. In an instant I was transported back to an acid trip including colors. I rebuked it, making a declaration that it had no hold on me AT ALL. In that second, the flashback was gone, never to return. God in the flesh (mine), making darkness into light, ever gracious, ever compassionate, and ever righteous. The light of God dispels every darkness. My heart trusts Him. So does yours.

February 03

Our soul has escaped as a bird out of the snare of the trapper;

The snare is broken and we have escaped.

Our help is in the name of the Lord,

Who made heaven and earth.

Psalm 124:7-8

NOTE: It doesn't say, "Our help is in the Lord."

Can you imagine what power and might and HELP there is in His very NAME?

I don't often think of my life before Christ but when I do, it is always with a sense of gratefulness and relief. So many things because of Jesus, I've been able to escape, dodge, and lay down when I've called upon His Name. BC fear was a constant companion. When Jesus came into my life even that was dealt with. Since then I've had a Helper whose Name is the Lord. He's the One who made heaven and earth. I'm ever so grateful we have the same Helper.

February 04

He sent a man before them,

Joseph, *who* was sold as a slave.

They forced his feet into shackles,

He was put in irons;

Until the time that his word came to pass,

The word of the Lord refined him.

Psalm 105:17-19

There have been times when I've felt that I was 'put in shackles.' Not a pleasant place to be. Reflecting on those times is significantly better than actually being there. I've badgered God as to the 'why' when I've been in the irons, I admit it. Maybe Joseph did too and it seems as though he did not become bitter nor did he hate God as a result of his circumstances. As a matter of fact, he allowed God's Word to refine him in the midst of it. That's a good lesson for me to hear, even in old age. In each instance of my past, His direction, His Word, has brought life to me and yep, I've been and am being refined by it. Same goes for you, I'm pretty sure.

February 05

Simon Peter, a bond-servant and apostle of Jesus Christ,

To those who have received a faith of the same kind as ours, by the righteousness of our God and Savior, Jesus Christ: Grace and peace be multiplied to you in the knowledge of God and of Jesus our Lord; seeing that His divine power has granted to us everything pertaining to life and godliness, through the true knowledge of Him who called us by His own glory and excellence.

2 Peter 1:1-3

NOTE: this is the only place in the Scripture that uses the term "His divine power."

It's interesting that the writer first puts a value on faith and those around him, and it is to them, that he's writing. Hmmm. Might it be that he's speaking to those specifically whose understanding of this faith he speaks of is the same as his? He then refers to specifics (grace and peace) being multiplied in the knowledge of God and Jesus....SEEING that HIS DIVINE POWER has granted us EVERYTHING pertaining to life and godliness, once again through the TRUE KNOWLEDGE of Him who called us! And what did He call us to? To His own glory and virtue, that's what!

February 06

Answer me when I call, O God of my righteousness!
You have relieved me in my distress;
Be gracious to me and hear my prayer.
But know that the Lord has set apart the godly man for Himself;
The Lord hears when I call to Him.

Psalm 4:1, 3

The literal translation of vs. 1 says:
Answer me when I call, Oh God who maintains my righteousness,
You have made room for me in my distress;
Be gracious to me and hear my prayer.
I love to read the Psalms David wrote. He has the assurance/faith to say: "Answer me when I call, O God of my righteousness.
You make room for me in my distress."
He then makes the declaration, "the Lord has set apart the godly man for Himself"! .....and then, "The Lord hears when I call to Him."

Here's the order:

Answer me.
You make room for my distress! (AMEN!)
You've set me apart for you.
You hear me when I call.

David's heart toward God is simply outstanding. I want to know God in THAT way, to have that same assurance to be able to say, "Answer me oh God, relieve my distress, You've set ME apart for you! HEAR me when I call!" It's my prayer for you too!

February 07

Therefore, since we receive a kingdom which cannot be shaken, let us show gratitude, by which we may offer to God an acceptable service with reverence and awe; for our God is a consuming fire.

Hebrews 12:28-29

For me, it's at the end of the day when gratitude is the most essential and particularly the most difficult to come by. It's not when laying in a bed of roses but rather when a thorn has pushed into my skin. It's when, in my eyes, I haven't enough or perhaps have too much or I just want to whine about something. That is when showing reverent fear is an acceptable service, the truly deep respect with which I revere God. Those are the precious times and I need them. So do you.

February 08

For a child will be born to us, a son will be given to us; And the government will rest on His shoulders; And His name will be called Wonderful Counselor, Mighty God, Eternal Father, Prince of Peace. There will be no end to the increase of *His* government or of peace, On the throne of David and over his kingdom, To establish it and to uphold it with justice and righteousness From then on and forevermore. The zeal of the Lord of hosts will accomplish this.

Isaiah 9:6-7

I just wanted to remind everyone of the 'end game.' We have a Wonderful Counselor, a Mighty God, an Eternal Father, and a Prince of Peace who has been given ALL AUTHORITY. We have Him! We also have the promise that there will be NO END to the increase of HIS government or of peace. He will hold it up with justice and righteousness FOREVERMORE!

......AND it is HIS zeal that will accomplish it! What an endgame! It's like money in the bank that never tarnishes nor may be stolen or taken away!

February 09

It is well with the man who is gracious and lends;

He will maintain his cause in judgment.

For he will never be shaken;

The righteous will be remembered forever.

Psalm 112:5-6

Back in Minnesota, I lived in a neighborhood where no one locked their doors (I still don't). When someone needed a tool, or really anything else, one simply helped themselves, even if the neighbor wasn't home. It wasn't a big deal. Everyone knew the arrangement and everyone honored it. I remember those days fondly and love them, as do our sons I believe. Everyone's kids wandered the neighborhood too. Again, there was a trust level that in thinking about it, was a delight. Pretty sure that's the way God intended it to be. He's the scorekeeper anyway. It truly is He who is the giver and the taker, and oh what a grand job He does!

February 10

Therefore be patient, brethren, until the coming of the Lord. The farmer waits for the precious produce of the soil, being patient about it, until it gets the early and late rains. You too be patient; strengthen your hearts, for the coming of the Lord is near.

James 5:7-8

What this DOESN'T say is "let 'God' strengthen your hearts during the wait." We are called to strengthen our own hearts, to be patient! It's called "delayed gratification" in child-raising terms. Learning to wait, to encourage ourselves, produces endurance and strength in our souls. He's coming and we know it! May patience and strength prevail!

February 11

Arise, O Lord, do not let man prevail; Let the nations be judged before You.

Put them in fear, O Lord; Let the nations know that they are but men. *Selah.*

Psalm 9:19-20

There is but one who judges righteously and His Name is above every Name. To fear Him with a reverent fear is good. It is like the sun spoken of in Malachi 4, the sun with healing in its wings, burning away the chaff.

February 12

Who is the man who fears the Lord?

He will instruct him in the way he should choose.

His soul will abide in prosperity,

And his descendants will inherit the land.

Psalm 25:12-13

So FIRST God instructs us in the way we should choose.

Next, we have the promise that our *soul* will abide (live) in prosperity (defined as a successful, flourishing, or thriving condition) AND our descendants will inherit the land. Period. That's what it says.

My soul does live in that place and my descendants WILL inherit the land and because it is from God, it is and will continue to be, a good land, a good inheritance! AMEN! Same goes for you.

February 13

Rejoice always; pray without ceasing; in everything give thanks; for this is God's will for you in Christ Jesus. Do not quench the Spirit; do not despise prophetic utterances. But examine everything *carefully*; hold fast to that which is good; abstain from every form of evil.

1 Thessalonians 5:16-22

One must be 'careful' with this Scripture! Folks get angry when they're in a bad place (I speak from experience) and someone tells them to, "...give thanks; for this is God's will for you in Christ Jesus." This then is about walking by faith. This is a truth for life! If we as God's people get the first four, I'm pretty sure the rest of the instructions will come about as the fruit of those first ones!

February 14

Teach me to do Your will,

For You are my God;

Let Your good Spirit lead me on level ground.

Psalm 143:10

My dad owned a farm for a short time that was very hilly, unlike his previous farm. I remember how much he hated it, yearning once again to be on level ground. No terracing required. No drama. Level ground. A sameness that one can depend upon. Good Spirit, lead me and mine on level ground. Same for the rest of you too.

February 15

"He who offers a sacrifice of thanksgiving honors Me;

And to him who orders *his* way *aright*

I shall show the salvation of God."

Psalm 50:23

I have used this 'thought' but once and yet it defines who I am in Christ; what I stand on. To be totally honest, it is an aggravation to offer thanksgiving to Him at times for what I don't understand. It is a pain to honor Him with thanksgiving when I am sick or 'sick' of a situation or what has been thrown my way. And yet...in the doing of it...in making the sacrifice of thanksgiving to Him in the midst of whatever circumstance I find myself, by the ordering of my way toward HIM, His response is to give me my very salvation! Oh, Glory be to God! He doesn't stop there though; He gives ever so much more.

February 16

Now may the God who gives perseverance and encouragement grant you to be of the same mind with one another according to Christ Jesus, so that with one accord you may with one voice glorify the God and Father of our Lord Jesus Christ.

Now may the God of hope fill you with all joy and peace in believing, so that you will abound in hope by the power of the Holy Spirit.

Romans 15:5-6, 13

So I gotta tell ya, there seems to be some people that I need the perseverance to be of the same mind with! I may need a bit of encouragement too. Pretty sure they feel the same way. It's available for us! It says so RIGHT HERE! The thing is, the goal itself truly is one that burns away the difficulty like chaff in the wind. It is to glorify God, the Father of our Lord Jesus Christ! AMEN and AMEN!

February 17

Let your speech always be with grace, *as though* seasoned with salt, so that you will know how you should respond to each person.

Colossians 4:6

Sarcasm is my go-to place. It's what comes most naturally to me. I think it and then I say it. Ugghh. The only way I know how to speak with grace on my lips is to really be in constant communication with the Holy Spirit, to listen to that still small voice that tells me when to keep still or to flavor my words with peace instead of anger, with wisdom instead of sarcasm, SO THAT I build up and not tear down so that I give instead of take. It is a good lesson to learn. Did you know that salt is used to season because it reduces bitterness?

February 18

Let us not lose heart in doing good, for in due time we will reap if we do not grow weary. So then, while we have opportunity, let us do good to all people, and especially to those who are of the household of the faith.

Galatians 6:9-10

If I have an annoyance and trust me, I do, it is this topic. This is one of those 'important' Scriptures I felt essential to impart to our sons. We give as others need and we DO NOT EXPECT REPAYMENT FROM THEM, NOR DO WE KEEP TRACK!

No hard feelings, no guilt. God gives a better return anyway! He also gives back more than we've given AND HE is the One who makes even, every score!

February 19

Both riches and honor *come* from You, and You rule over all, and in Your hand is power and might; and it lies in Your hand to make great and to strengthen everyone. Now therefore, our God, we thank You, and praise Your glorious name.

1 Chronicles 29:12-13

"Everyone" is us, folks! Our inheritance is to be strengthened and to be made great! Hard to believe huh? Truth! In the walking out of that truth, it is good to thank God, to praise His glorious Name!

February 20

The Lord God has given Me the tongue of disciples,

That I may know how to sustain the weary one with a word.

He awakens Me morning by morning,

He awakens My ear to listen as a disciple.

Isaiah 50:4

Isaiah speaks this word prophetically, pointing to Jesus Christ. It was for then and it is for now. There is that One who sustains the weary with a word and I am forever grateful to have heard it and to keep hearing it, now and forever. Methinks the same goes for you. NOTE: The 'listening' part is important too.

February 21

Trust in the Lord with all your heart

And do not lean on your own understanding.

In all your ways acknowledge Him,

And He will make your paths straight.

Proverbs 3:5-6

A number of years ago God took something from me that He'd given me. I was angry (He can handle that by the way), bummed, disappointed, and generally despondent for a while. You know though....life goes on, right? He gets to do what He wants. He is, after all, God and He's what I signed up for. In this case, my 'own understanding' was completely absent. I could come up with a few ideas as to the 'why' but none seemed to fit the bill at the time. I did get the 'lean not on your own understanding' part. I really did. I did not become hard-hearted though I wanted to. I love Him more than I love bitterness and that's where my mind could easily have taken me.

Flash forward. Because of that 'taking away' my horizons have changed as has my faith. I wouldn't have chosen to go where He's led me but the fruit of the journey has worked steel into my soul and it has been good for both me and my family. He has expanded the place of my tent. You know it's always about Him. His faithfulness is ever true. My path has been made straight and so has yours.

February 22

Your throne is established from of old;

You are from everlasting.

Your testimonies are fully confirmed;

Holiness befits Your house,

O Lord, forevermore.

Psalm 93:2, 5

The leader and most would say, the tyrant of Uzbekistan died. He ruled for twenty-seven years. His 'throne' had been established. When he left, it left.

Our God's throne was established from of old and LASTS FOREVER. Our God's testimonies are fully confirmed AND His HOLINESS BENEFITS OUR HOUSE FOREVER! His holiness benefits ME, FOREVER! YOU TOO!

February 23

The *former* priests, on the one hand, existed in greater numbers because they were prevented by death from continuing, but Jesus, on the other hand, because He continues forever, holds His priesthood permanently. Therefore He is able also to save forever those who draw near to God through Him, since He always lives to make intercession for them.

Hebrews 7:23-25

Though at times it seems that the power of hell is beating at my door, there is ONE who stands in the way, who holds me before the Father to work on my behalf! Now THAT is REAL POWER!

I have a Priest who saves FOREVER. He continually lives to make intercession for ME. With Him for me, who can stand against me? Same goes for you.

February 24

I was reading Ezra this morning pertaining to the story of his leading his people to Jerusalem. He says:

For I was ashamed to request from the king troops and horsemen to protect us from the enemy on the way, because we had said to the king, "The hand of our God is favorably disposed to all those who seek Him, but His power and His anger are against all those who forsake Him." So we fasted and sought our God concerning this *matter*, and He listened to our entreaty.

Ezra 8:22-23

Ezra had to put his money where his mouth was, so to speak. How often I boast of what God is able to do and then drop the ball. May I and we as the people of God press into His Presence, to seek Him concerning a matter; to entreat Him to show in the flesh, that He is what we've said He is and He does what we've said He'd do! He's up to the task, trust me.

February 25

And every created thing which is in heaven and on the earth and under the earth and on the sea, and all things in them, I heard saying,

"To Him who sits on the throne, and to the Lamb, *be* blessing and honor and glory and dominion forever and ever."

Revelation 5:13

I've had this 'thought' three times in all the years I've been sending it. Once in 2010, and twice more in very quick succession. I pay attention to how and when I use a 'thought.' Here spelled out for me, is exactly what I expect and long for: EVERY SINGLE THING CREATED, everywhere, will declare blessing and honor and glory and dominion to HIM, who sits on the throne!

I can't read this Scripture without crying. I am undone in the Presence of God. It is that throne which I look to. Just so you know, I am bringing you along with me.

February 26

On God my salvation and my glory *rest*;

The rock of my strength, my refuge is in God.

Trust in Him at all times, O people;

Pour out your heart before Him;

God is a refuge for us. *Selah.*

Psalm 62:7-8

Over the years I've heard many pastors, teachers, believers speak of salvation through Jesus Christ. I get it. I do. I know truly that my salvation rests on Him. My glory though, I can't say I've heard anyone speak of.

If my glory rests on Him (and it does), what calamity can disgrace me or bring dishonor upon me? Here then, is the enabling power for my heart to trust Him. He has my back. He has yours too.

February 27

For in hope we have been saved, but hope that is seen is not hope; for who hopes for what he *already* sees? But if we hope for what we do not see, with perseverance we wait eagerly for it.

Romans 8:24-25

The granddaughter of some very dear friends of ours has died of inoperable cancer. The family in the midst of loss has this hope. With perseverance, steady persistence, in spite of grief, they have been called to hope in this saving, this Savior. I know that they eagerly wait and long for it! So do I and so do you.

February 28

Through Him then, let us continually offer up a sacrifice of praise to God, that is, the fruit of lips that give thanks to His name. And do not neglect doing good and sharing, for with such sacrifices God is pleased.

Hebrews 13:15-16

I was struck this morning by God equating praise to Him, doing good and sharing all, as sacrifices. I've always thought doing good and sharing are works, sacrificial perhaps. Praising Him is a sacrifice too? It's defined as "the surrender of something prized or desirable for the sake of something considered having a higher or more pressing claim." This puts "praise to Him" in a whole new light. His IS the higher, the more pressing claim!

February 29

Your kingdom is an everlasting kingdom,

And Your dominion *endures* throughout all generations.

Psalm 145:13

AND

"Listen to Me, you who know righteousness,

A people in whose heart is My law;

Do not fear the reproach of man,

Nor be dismayed at their revilings.

"For the moth will eat them like a garment,

And the grub will eat them like wool.

But My righteousness will be forever,

And My salvation to all generations."

Isaiah 51:7-8

I was just thinking today that my sons have had a better start at 'life' than I did. I do not boast here. I know who to give credit to for it and His Name is Jesus Christ. Each of them has had his own trials, his own difficulties to work through, his own 'refiner's fire' if you will. There is a Rock they've grown accustomed to standing on though and it will not be swayed or washed away. If I hope for anything, it is that they cling to that Rock and pass along the knowing of that salvation to their children. I've laid claim to them, every one of them...

March

March 01

For God did not send the Son into the world to judge the world, but that the world might be saved through Him. He who believes in Him is not judged; he who does not believe has been judged already, because he has not believed in the name of the only begotten Son of God. This is the judgment, that the Light has come into the world, and men loved the darkness rather than the Light, for their deeds were evil. For everyone who does evil hates the Light, and does not come to the Light for fear that his deeds will be exposed. But he who practices the truth comes to the Light, so that his deeds may be manifested as having been wrought in God."

John 3:17-21

There are many names of evil. Shame and fear are but a few. I've owned most of them. God changed my heart though and I don't have to 'own' any of them anymore. Neither do you!

March 02

You who fear the Lord, trust in the Lord;

He is their help and their shield.

He will bless those who fear the Lord,

The small together with the great.

Psalm 115:11, 13

Can someone be helped who's hiding behind a shield? It depends upon who's holding it up; how much they are trusted. This is exactly the crux of the matter for me. It's that 'trust' issue again. The meager faith that I have sometimes fools me into believing He's let down His guard, lowered the shield covering me, so to speak. The good news is; His ability to hold it up, never waivers and it doesn't depend upon my belief! I trust Him and that absolutely is enough! His blessings are upon me and upon you too!

March 03

"Ask, and it will be given to you; seek, and you will find; knock, and it will be opened to you. For everyone who asks receives, and he who seeks finds, and to him who knocks it will be opened.

Matthew 7:7-8

You've heard the saying; "How badly do you want it?" I'm pretty sure that applies here.

The literal translation of this Scripture matters. It says:

Keep asking and it will be given to you; keep seeking and you will find; keep knocking and it will be opened to you. There is a consistency here that needs to be maintained. The world calls it delayed gratification which isn't all bad. I call it faith.

March 04

Enter His gates with thanksgiving

And His courts with praise.

Give thanks to Him, bless His name.

For the Lord is good;

His lovingkindness is everlasting

And His faithfulness to all generations.

Psalm 100:4-5

I enter His courts most of the time asking for something. Well, I give thanks too but to enter, step into His Presence with praise on my lips, not nearly enough. Give thanks to Him, bless His Holy Name! That is what He asks of me! What do I get in return? I get to have a Father who is forever good, whose lovingkindness is everlasting, and who is forever faithful to me, to my children, to my children's children down through the ages into eternity! I can hardly imagine!

I am who I am because of who He is. I am not who I would have been without Him. Same goes for you.

March 05

For the word of God is living and active and sharper than any two-edged sword, and piercing as far as the division of soul and spirit, of both joints and marrow, and able to judge the thoughts and intentions of the heart.

Hebrews 4:12

Jeremiah 23:29 says of the Word of God: "Is not My word like fire?" declares the LORD, "and like a hammer which shatters a rock?" This is that same Word of God that dwells within us! This is the very same Word of God that Paul makes reference to in Ephesians 6, calling it the sword of the Spirit! "....take the HELMET OF SALVATION, and the sword of the Spirit which is the WORD OF GOD."

I'm pretty sure you get this folks. May the Word of God on our lips pierce where it is required, to heal and bring life. We are called to 'sharpen' each other with the Word of God, not to tear down but rather to bring clarity to those things that would seek to bring confusion, hurt, and anguish.

If we then have this living, active, sharp sword of the Spirit living within us, at our beck and call, let's use it!

March 06

Surely our griefs He Himself bore,

And our sorrows He carried;

Yet we ourselves esteemed Him stricken,

Smitten of God, and afflicted.

But He was pierced through for our transgressions,

He was crushed for our iniquities;

The chastening for our well-being *fell* upon Him,

And by His scourging we are healed.

Isaiah 53:4-5

Sometimes in the early morning as I'm praying on the way to work....I'm just simply tired, grief-stricken. Whether at times it's physical or mental, I just am exhausted. It's especially then that I simply give what I'm carrying to Him. I verbally give it to Him to carry for me, and you know something? HE takes my grief, my sorrow, my sins, my sense of hopelessness...and gives me peace and healing in return, EVERY SINGLE TIME, on the spot. Same goes for you. Just ask.

March 07

A stone is heavy and the sand weighty, But the provocation of a fool is heavier than both of them.

Proverbs 27:3

Provocation: something that incites, instigates, angers, or irritates.

We all carry baggage, some more and some less. It at times causes us to be plain nasty and foolish, to push buttons that would be better left alone. I'm making no excuses for neither me nor you. I'm saying that there's a way around it, a way to toss the heavy stone away.

Wars start because of the goading of fools. Provocation comes squarely between a person's being able to hear God and listening to the worthless chatter of someone who seeks on behalf of themselves. May the speech of each of us be seasoned with everything good.

March 08

Let no unwholesome word proceed from your mouth, but only such *a word* as is good for edification according to the need *of the moment*, so that it will give grace to those who hear.

Ephesians 4:29

The word 'unwholesome' here means literally 'rotten.' When something is rotten, it spreads rot. I like to believe on occasion that I extend grace (as I think of those instances where I'm perturbed with someone/something), where I don't rant and rave but rather keep my mouth shut. This though is taking that a huge step further. It is allowing the Holy Spirit to give such clarity to a situation, that what comes out of my mouth edifies, gives grace, at exactly the moment when needed! The dictionary defines grace as a pleasing or attractive endowment: favor or goodwill. This then is what takes the 'me' out of grace and puts in the 'HE.' You too methinks.

March 09

Grace to you and peace from God our Father and the Lord Jesus Christ, who gave Himself for our sins so that He might rescue us from this present evil age, according to the will of our God and Father, to whom *be* the glory forevermore. Amen.

Galatians 1:3-5

The definition of rescue:

To free or deliver from confinement, violence, danger, or evil.

He HAS rescued me. He's rescued you also and if He hasn't, it's because you haven't asked Him. Now's a good time. It lasts forever too.

March 10

Cast your burden upon the Lord and He will sustain you;

He will never allow the righteous to be shaken.

Psalm 55:22

It says that He will never allow me to be shaken. It says He will sustain me. He will keep me from giving way by bearing my burdens. It doesn't say that He won't allow circumstances to happen which will cause me to have burdens.

For some reason this reminds me of a song my dear friend Mimi was in the process of writing a long time ago, singing it to me. One of the lines goes...."You are my Captain, and You calm the angry sea...You are my Captain and my King." This is a perfect analogy for me. He calms my angry sea, keeping me still on the water but removing the angry part.

Pretty sure it's the same with you.

March 11

There is one body and one Spirit, just as also you were called in one hope of your calling; one Lord, one faith, one baptism, one God and Father of all who is over all and through all and in all. But to each one of us grace was given according to the measure of Christ's gift.

Ephesians 4:4-7

We ALL have one Lord, one hope, one faith, one baptism, one God and Father. We all live in the same house folks. Note here: It doesn't say, "We were ALL given grace." It says, "...to EACH ONE of us", individually and exactly the grace we require is given to us, according to the measure of Christ's gift. Sometimes I need more grace than you do, to walk the walk. He's right there and gives it to me every single time. You too! How cool is that!

March 12

For everyone who partakes *only* of milk is not accustomed to the word of righteousness, for he is an infant. But solid food is for the mature, who because of practice have their senses trained to discern good and evil.

Hebrews 5:13-14

I've never used this 'thought' before. Just this once. Milk is the beginning of acquiring one's taste. It's rather bland and for the most part, it's liked or at least tolerated because it's really all one gets from birth to about six months. Then though, one's sense of taste begins to mature. Following this analogy, parents at the beginning, shove in stuff that isn't particularly liked but is good to grow on! When one is older, one puts in yes of course, what is good. There must also be a bit of that 'shoving in' part to maintain oneself in a healthy manner. To know what to 'shove in' is indeed the result of one's discernment.

March 13

The words of the wise heard in quietness are *better* than the shouting of a ruler among fools.

Ecclesiastes 9:17

It doesn't say, "The words of the wise spoken in quietness..."

I can't listen when I'm talking. Some of the best times I've had with the Lord are in my 'quiet' times. It's when I've said my piece and simply shut up long enough to hear what He has to say. It's the same with people. Sometimes I decide whomever I'm with isn't wise and I don't listen. Sometimes I think I know better and don't listen and sometimes, I just don't want to listen even though I know the speaker is yes, wise. Words spoken with wisdom ARE better than shouting among fools! I'm working on the listening part. Same with you?

March 14

Opening his mouth, Peter said: "I most certainly understand *now* that God is not one to show partiality, but in every nation the man who fears Him and does what is right is welcome to Him.

Acts 10:34-35

I was 'fretting' again this morning as I prayed on my way to work. What to pray? Where to turn? Still in fretting mode, as I sat down to read Scriptures to seek out the 'thought' for today I really heard the still, small voice of the Holy Spirit say,

"I've got this."

...and you know, He DOES! I am WELCOME to Him! I have been given full rights to Him! He's got my back, He covers me, He heals me and you know, He's got my country too, not for my plans but for His plans! He's GOT THIS! Either I believe it or I don't. Faith in action!

March 15

"You shall not take the name of the Lord your God in vain, for the Lord will not leave him unpunished who takes His name in vain.

Exodus 20:7

This is pretty simple, right? In school, kids are continually saying, "Oh my god!" (with a small g). Now they don't say goddammit, but nevertheless, in my office, I have this rule. I don't let them say "Oh my god!" This has sparked a number of conversations over the years, to the point that when someone says it, other students that know me, will correct them by usually saying something like, "You can't say that in here."

I like that.

My thought here is that I don't appreciate it at all when someone uses my name harshly. It makes me feel small inside. Our God isn't small, He's just. He doesn't allow it and neither will I.

March 16

The Lord nullifies the counsel of the nations;

He frustrates the plans of the peoples.

The counsel of the Lord stands forever,

The plans of His heart from generation to generation.

Blessed is the nation whose God is the Lord,

The people whom He has chosen for His own inheritance.

Psalm 33:10-12

I typically scan a couple hundred Twitter accounts very early every morning. I'm not looking for 'Believers' accounts, I'm doing it for a few businesses. So many of the individual account holders though, in a few succinct words, declare their belief in Jesus Christ. Don't believe it when you hear murmurs of "The US is a post-Christian nation." Not true. This nation is one who has millions that declare that God IS THE LORD! WE are whom He has chosen for His own inheritance! He will nullify the counsel of the nations and He will frustrate the plans of the peoples to give US a HOPE and a FUTURE!

March 17

"As for me, I know that my Redeemer lives,

And at the last He will take His stand on the earth.

"Even after my skin is destroyed,

Yet from my flesh I shall see God;

Whom I myself shall behold,

And whom my eyes will see and not another.

My heart faints within me!

Job 19:25-28

During most of my years working at a school, I had this 'thought' sitting along with a few others on my desk on one of those photo cubes. I never made mention of it because of course one 'couldn't' but very often I reflected upon it as my eyes would lay hold of it. If a student asked about it, and some did...I was able to talk a bit about it, which of course, I did.

It's one of the two Scriptures that I have claimed, stood on, and believed over my fifty year walk with God. This is money in my bank. It is every single thing I hope and believe for. THIS is the God I serve! He lives and I for one, am so grateful that I found it out! At the last He WILL take His stand on the earth. I'll be there right along with him and so will you.

March 18

Let me hear Your lovingkindness in the morning;

For I trust in You;

Teach me the way in which I should walk;

For to You I lift up my soul.

Psalm 143:8

I am a morning 'fearful' person. I don't wake up trusting. As a matter of fact, I fairly frequently wake up from difficult dreams....finding myself in places where I'm either in fear or at the very least uncomfortable. It takes me a few minutes to mentally adjust, to have that 'aha' moment when I realize that I am cocooned in the trust of Him who knows my name. Every single morning He lifts up my soul.

Every. single. morning.

It's the same with you. I know it.

March 19

How precious is Your lovingkindness, O God!

And the children of men take refuge in the shadow of Your wings.

They drink their fill of the abundance of Your house; And You give them to drink of the river of Your delights.

For with You is the fountain of life;

In Your light we see light.

Psalm 36:7-9

Most people think I'm brave but I am not. Foolhardy perhaps but not brave. So often I've found myself hunkered down in the shadow of His wings. It is a wonderful place to be, let me tell you. There are no prerequisites for going there either. It is that place too, where there truly is an abundance, where water is plentiful and it's the sort which quenches my body and my soul of thirst.

We are to drink that water until we are FULL! Funny thing about being full. It gives one an entirely different perspective!

March 20

Beloved, do not imitate what is evil, but what is good. The one who does good is of God; the one who does evil has not seen God.

3 John 1:11

I wouldn't have chosen this 'thought' as it seems rather obvious to me (I'm a VERY black and white person). Nevertheless, here it is! The thing that strikes me is that it doesn't say, "...do not do evil, but what is good." It rather says, "...do not 'imitate' what is evil." There is a 'seeing' or 'hearing' of those around us that we are to pay attention to so as not to imitate. Here then is one of those times where we may practice righteousness, for the sake of what is good!

This is pretty easy for me with the big stuff. Not so much for the little stuff sometimes though. Speaking kindly, believing the best, forgiving as I want to be forgiven. Lots of things that I need to give Him to carry for me and through the giving, I am good in Him. You get the picture. Same goes for you!

March 21

Let the words of my mouth and the meditation of my heart

Be acceptable in Your sight,

O Lord, my rock and my Redeemer.

Psalm 19:14

This 'thought' has made many visits to my 'thought' for the day which I've sent out over the years. There's a reason it keeps reappearing.

Sue's paraphrase:

Please help me to keep my mouth shut unless it is to speak what is good. Let me think on what is good instead of vain imaginings so that I may please you Father. You are my Lord, You are my Rock and You most certainly are the one charged with the duty of restoring my rights and avenging the wrongs done to me so that I don't need to take it upon myself to do it.

"Oh God, help me to keep this 'filter' on my mouth." Yours too dear reader.

March 22

As for me, I shall call upon God,
And the Lord will save me.
Evening and morning and at noon, I will complain and
murmur,
And He will hear my voice.

Psalm 55:16-17

Recently I had to pick up twelve lbs of raw honey. The pickup point was quite a distance from my car and it was slick and icy. Coming back to the car was an incline. As I was carrying the box I passed a number of guys and as each passed me by I thought that had it been one of my sons, they would have immediately asked if they could carry the box. The jars inside the box were made of glass and I was fearful of dropping them, not to mention that I was pretty annoyed. Then I thought to myself, well I could ask for help but my pride just wouldn't let me. When I was literally ten steps away from my car a guy just arriving, asked if he could help. "No, I'm almost at my car, but thanks anyway." was my reply.

I sat in the car for a bit, feeling fairly miffed at God. "You could have sent someone to help me! The load was too heavy and too clumsy for me to carry."

"You could have asked for help." that still small voice replied.

Sometimes I don't ask because I don't have the faith to believe He can help. Sometimes I think I can handle it myself and have to come to the point that I am exhausted and cry out in desperation and then there are those few times when, out of a love I have for Him and faith which knows that He will make my burden light and not allow me to be shaken, those times I simply trust Him and hand Him the load. You too?

March 23

For though we walk in the flesh, we do not war according to the flesh, for the weapons of our warfare are not of the flesh, but divinely powerful for the destruction of fortresses. *We are* destroying speculations and every lofty thing raised up against the knowledge of God, and *we are* taking every thought captive to the obedience of Christ

2 Corinthians 10:3-5

Who believes that? Who of us believes that the war we face isn't of the flesh and that the weapons at our disposal are divinely powerful for the destruction of fortresses? Who believes that we can take EVERY THOUGHT captive to the obedience of Christ? When one does believe it, it's like money in the bank. One can stand on it and lay hold of it.

Walking in the power of God means to destroy 'speculations' and replace them with faith. It means to decide not to believe knowledge coming from the world of sin and death which goes against of knowledge of God. It means taking captive those thoughts of unbelief and rather standing firm in ones' belief in Christ. He gave us the weapons of warfare for a purpose.

March 24

Those who love Your law have great peace,

And nothing causes them to stumble.

Psalm 119:165

This 'thought' speaks to me a bit differently perhaps than to most folks. Some could believe it to mean that to struggle, to have a difficult time is to be lacking in this faith, this peace; thereby meaning one must accept a sort of forced/coerced peace, grudging and contrived which doesn't have much reality to it when difficulty comes.

Quite the contrary! To me, this speaks of a place. A place I go when I read the 'Word,' when I meditate on the reality of who God is in my life. I'm not always in that place but I know that I can always get there...in an instant. It is a place where there is no stumbling because I know who I'm leaning on. I can trust Him to steer my ship, to listen to me, and hear me when there is no one else I can speak to. I love that place and I love Him. Nothing truly can make me stumble. You either.

March 25

"I am the Alpha and the Omega," says the Lord God, "who is and who was and who is to come, the Almighty."

Revelation 1:8

He is who He says He is and He does what He says He'll do. I want to encourage each of you, me (too!) that as we walk out our daily lives, we maintain a holiness, that we keep our thoughts and our mouths in check. That we bless rather than curse, that we walk by His might and not by ours. The last line of the above 'thought' literally says, "who is and who was and who is coming, the Almighty." He is COMING and on that day, we will hear those words, "thou good and faithful servant." It's all Him folks.

March 26

"But for you who fear My name, the sun of righteousness will rise with healing in its wings; and you will go forth and skip about like calves from the stall.

Malachi 4:2

One translation reads:

"But for you who revere My name, the sun of a dawn without clouds will rise with healing in its wings; and you will go forth and skip about like calves from the stall."

Every one of us needs healing. Some from being hurt by unforgiveness, some by sorrow, some by an illness, and some by having been wounded. There is a promise, a Word that God has given each of us that declares that HE brings healing like the dawn without clouds so that we are able to GO FORTH! We are able to skip about like calves from the stall! It is THAT dawn, THAT skipping that heals us, that brings relief!

March 27

Unless the Lord builds the house,

They labor in vain who build it;

Unless the Lord guards the city,

The watchman keeps awake in vain.

Psalm 127:1

I've only used this 'thought' once. Hmmmm, and yet it has been what I've stood on since the day I met Him. May I be so bold as to use it both on a personal level and on a national level? There is power in this Word! The Lord Jesus IS the One who has BUILT the house, the nation and me. He is the One who is greater than any watchman! It's a trust issue.

He's built the house, the city, the nation. We get to choose where we live.

March 28

O my strength, I will sing praises to You;

For God is my stronghold,

The God who shows me lovingkindness.

Psalm 59:17

I can't believe it! I was considering singing to the Lord and what a joy it brings to my heart, also to His heart, when I happened upon this Word.

Stronghold has two distinct meanings here. I believe both apply to the verse above:

A well-fortified place; fortress.

A place that serves as the center of a group, as of militants or of persons holding a controversial viewpoint:

Is HE a place to go that is secure, a well-fortified fortress? Is HE a place that is the center of a group of people holding a controversial viewpoint (especially in these days)? Yep!

So.....I SHALL sing praises to Him! May we all join the choir!

March 29

"Behold, God is my salvation,
I will trust and not be afraid;
For the Lord God is my strength and song,
And He has become my salvation."
Therefore you will joyously draw water
From the springs of salvation.
And in that day you will say,
"Give thanks to the Lord,
Call on His name.
Make known His deeds among the peoples;
Make them remember that His name is exalted."

Isaiah 12:2-4

I've been thinking about how often I have lived/done this Word. I get wrapped up in my own little world and I forget that I'm here to do His will.

"Make known His deeds among the peoples; make them remember that His Name is exalted." The payback of course is salvation, strength and living water!

It bears repeating:

"....make them remember that His Name is exalted,"

March 30

Then the sons of Judah drew near to Joshua in Gilgal, and Caleb the son of Jephunneh the Kenizzite said to him, "You know the word which the Lord spoke to Moses the man of God concerning you and me in Kadesh-barnea. I was forty years old when Moses the servant of the Lord sent me from Kadesh-barnea to spy out the land, and I brought word back to him as *it was* in my heart. Nevertheless my brethren who went up with me made the heart of the people melt with fear; but I followed the Lord my God fully. So Moses swore on that day, saying, 'Surely the land on which your foot has trodden will be an inheritance to you and to your children forever, because you have followed the Lord my God fully.' Now behold, the Lord has let me live, just as He spoke, these forty-five years, from the time that the Lord spoke this word to Moses, when Israel walked in the wilderness; and now behold, I am eighty-five years old today. I am still as strong today as I was in the day Moses sent me; as my strength was then, so my strength is now, for war and for going out and coming in. Now then, give me this hill country about which the Lord spoke on that day, for you heard on that day that Anakim *were* there, with great fortified cities; perhaps the Lord will be with me, and I will drive them out as the Lord has spoken."

So Joshua blessed him and gave Hebron to Caleb the son of Jephunneh for an inheritance. Therefore, Hebron became the inheritance of Caleb the son of Jephunneh the Kenizzite until this day, because he followed the Lord God of Israel fully.

Joshua 14.6-14

Forty-five years Caleb waited for the promise given to him to have his request fulfilled. During that time he did not falter in following the Lord. He did not become bitter and HE DID NOT QUIT BELIEVING FOR HIS INHERITANCE. Caleb was a man given to God and so are each of us! Take heart! We follow, He leads, we ask, He gives!

March 31

Jesus said to him, "I am the way, and the truth, and the life; no one comes to the Father but through Me.

John 14:6

Sue's translation:

I am the means for attaining the goal, I am the indisputable fact, I am the condition of existence; no one comes to the Father but through Me.

In the foot race of life, He's made it possible for me to win! He says it's an indisputable fact. Through Him I exist AND through Him, I am able to come to the Father, to the Throne of Grace, the finish line!

Oh the JOY! I WIN THE RACE! SO DO YOU!

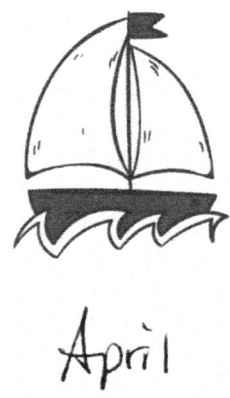

April

April 01

The title of this Psalm is: "A Citizen of Zion"

That's us folks!

O Lord, who may abide in Your tent?

Who may dwell on Your holy hill?

He who walks with integrity, and works righteousness,

And speaks truth in his heart.

Psalm 15:1-2

I do get the "walks with integrity, and works righteousness" part. For me, those are 'outward' things, outward actions one simply does because God has called us to do them. It's the part about "speaks truth in his heart" that is at times difficult for me. It isn't so much speaking 'truth' to others as it is 'speaking truth to me.' I tell myself that I'm offended with someone....instead of laying the offense down and giving it no place to reside in my heart. I tell myself I'm 'alone' when I have dear loved ones all around me who, at my request, would call me, seek me out. I tell myself that my value to God is in what I can do instead of who I am. I must choose to tell truths and believe those truths in my heart. Those truths lead to the very best place...His holy hill! Same goes for you.

April 02

Let all who seek You rejoice and be glad in You;

Let those who love Your salvation say continually,

"The Lord be magnified!"

Psalm 40:16

These are almost the same words David uses in Psalm 70. I love his Psalms. His is an eternal vision of what is important. I so often get in the "I need this" or "please do that" mode when I'm praying instead of asking Him what He needs, simply magnifying HIM and telling Him that I am so grateful that He came for me. He's given me the opportunity to be glad in Him FOREVER! That's a LONG time!

April 03

I solemnly charge *you* in the presence of God and of Christ Jesus, who is to judge the living and the dead, and by His appearing and His kingdom: preach the word; be ready in season *and* out of season; reprove, rebuke, exhort, with great patience and instruction.

2 Timothy 4:1-2

Not once, have I used this Scripture. Hmmm. It seems to me this can be interpreted just one way, no matter which Church/group one calls home. 'Be ready.'

A friend of my son teaches tactical protection classes. His mantra is to 'be ready.' It's the same for us as believers except that we get to do it with giving, helping, serving and yes of course, protecting.

Blessings on each of your heads over these days.

April 04

Finally, brethren, whatever is true, whatever is honorable, whatever is right, whatever is pure, whatever is lovely, whatever is of good repute, if there is any excellence and if anything worthy of praise, dwell on these things.

Philippians 4:8

A number of years ago I was 'strongly encouraged' to attend a training for my job, along with all staff members. It was on mindfulness and the first thing that happened was that the instructor hit a gong and asked us to empty our minds. I was so annoyed at the thought of 'emptying' what God had made full, that I stood up and walked out, went to my office and printed out these words without the Scripture reference. I pasted them to my office door and there they stood until the day I retired. I just might paste them on my door at home.

April 05

Sow your seed in the morning and do not be idle in the evening, for you do not know whether morning or evening sowing will succeed, or whether both of them alike will be good.

Ecclesiastes 11:6

I can do good in the morning. I can even do good at noon and in the afternoons. It's the evenings that are difficult. At night I think that I have the 'right' to stop doing good, to just do ME instead.

I had brought an uncompleted project home for my dear husband to work on, to finish the task for a student who didn't have the tools to complete the job. He had both prepared the way for my student to do a bit of work on it and then finished it! He completed the task and yes, it was in the evening! Most likely in the whole scheme of things that doesn't mean much. I know a boy though, that it meant a great deal to. There was much seed planted! It's the sowing on every single occasion, whether good or not good, rested or tired. That's what we're called to do! Sow your seed folks!

April 06

"Drip down, O heavens, from above, And let the clouds pour down righteousness; Let the earth open up and salvation bear fruit, And righteousness spring up with it. I, the Lord, have created it.

Isaiah 45:8

When one is truly thirsty, truly parched, an insistent, unending craving drives a person until that drink, that life-giving water has been obtained. That rain, that righteousness, must bear fruit in each of us. He created it that we might drink!

April 07

The name of the Lord is a strong tower;
The righteous runs into it and is safe.

Proverbs 18:10

The literal translation of this is:

The name of the Lord is a strong tower;

The righteous runs into it and is set on high.

I like that. His Name is a strong tower where I may go. It is where my view, my perspective changes. I no longer see from the ground but rather I am set on high with HIM as my foundation! That means I can't be shaken, even whilst being high up! I continually, always and forever, have that tower available to me too, that place which sets me above my worries, above my fears, and above those things that seek to keep me on the ground. That tower is HIM! You have the same tower too. I'll see you up there!

April 08

I have fought the good fight, I have finished the course, I have kept the faith; in the future there is laid up for me the crown of righteousness, which the Lord, the righteous Judge, will award to me on that day; and not only to me, but also to all who have loved His appearing.

2 Timothy 4:7-8

My parents gave me a thing which I cherish. It is the mindset to finish what I begin and it is a thing which every generation has to learn for themselves. This truth cuts across every avenue, every aspect of my life. It is a measurement that I can hold God accountable to as well. Stay the course, finish the race.

I know that it's important to you too and today, I want to encourage you that the fight is GOOD, we WILL KEEP THE FAITH and we WILL FINISH THE COURSE! God has finished His part. It's called the Resurrection of His Son. Now He's waiting on you and me.

April 09

"Cease *striving* and know that I am God; I will be exalted among the nations, I will be exalted in the earth."

The Lord of hosts is with us; The God of Jacob is our stronghold. *Selah*

Psalm 46:10-11

The literal translation of this is:

Let go, relax and know that I am God;

I will be exalted among the Gentiles,

I will be exalted in the earth."

The Lord of hosts is with us

The God of Jacob is our stronghold. *Selah*

Five things that I can't do very easily are all "let go and relax." It's the 'letting go' part that I'm not good at. It all comes down to faith. If I let go, will HE take control? Will the Lord of Hosts take up the slack? Will HE be my stronghold? Will HE accomplish that thing that I so desperately want to be able to have done or will HE meet that need that I don't know what to do about?

You know HE WILL! HE is with each of us! He is for us! HE is our stronghold! In HIM we can let go and relax!

April 10

For consider Him who has endured such hostility by sinners against Himself, so that you will not grow weary and lose heart.

Hebrews 12:3

Sickness leeches away a life. So too, does weariness. Of course, I know He died for me. I don't always call to mind though that He also endured hostility against Himself SO THAT I would NOT faint in my soul! He gave, I took. He gives, I take. I will NOT LOSE HEART! Neither will you!

April 11

Now as they were traveling along, He entered a village; and a woman named Martha welcomed Him into her home. She had a sister called Mary, who was seated at the Lord's feet, listening to His word. But Martha was distracted with much work; and she came up *to Him* and said, "Lord, do You not care that my sister has left me to do all the serving alone? Then tell her to help me." But the Lord answered and said to her, "Martha, Martha, you are worried and bothered about so many things; but *only* one thing is necessary, for Mary has chosen the good part, which shall not be taken away from her."

Luke 10:38-42

This Scripture has often annoyed me. I've been for Martha and just this morning it dawned on me what Martha was doing. She was keeping track. Mary was 'doing' less than she was. At our house we call it being a 'fairness whiner.' When we take it upon ourselves to 'keep track' we take it out of His hands. He's by far the better scorekeeper.

Here exactly is the dimension of the kingdom of God! When we keep track, we get exactly what we gave. When we let Him do it and simply serve HIM, the dimension of His kingdom comes into play. Give, and it will be given to you. They will pour into your lap a good measure—pressed down, shaken together, *and* running over. For by your standard of measure it will be measured to you in return.

May my measure ever be His measure! Yours too.

106

April 12

Light is sown *like seed* for the righteous

And gladness for the upright in heart.

Be glad in the Lord, you righteous ones,

And give thanks to His holy name.

Psalm 97:11-12

Here again, is my walk by faith. Do I believe this literally or is it just a good line? Has the light of God Himself been sown for me, whose righteousness I've been given? Gladness of heart has been sown in the soil of my heart? IF this is true, it is then my responsibility (there's always a cost isn't there?) to take it and make it mine! I MUST be glad in the Lord! I MUST give thanks for the memory of His Holy Name! It's the walking out of this, folks....that changes this 'thought' to life!

April 13

Do not let your heart envy sinners,

But *live* in the fear of the Lord always.

Surely there is a future,

And your hope will not be cut off.

Proverbs 23:17-18

Hmmm. I had this 'thought' only once before. I asked myself who exactly, do I envy? For me at least, it isn't folks with more money nor people in high places. It is rather those ones who are better than I am at doing a job. More specifically it is those whose level through my perfectionist-seeking eyes, I can never hope to match or reach.

Here's the thing though. Because I live in God ALWAYS, because through Him I have a future, it is through Him that my hope will NOT be cut off! It is through Him that I don't despair, nor ever am required to reach someone else's level, whatever that is...because in HIM I HAVE A FUTURE!! MY HOPE IS NOT CUT OFF!

This goes for you too dear ones!

April 14

Every good thing given and every perfect gift is from above, coming down from the Father of lights, with whom there is no variation or shifting shadow.

James 1:17

I woke up with this Scripture on my mind this morning. I like the part about "every perfect gift" and there being "no variation or shifting shadow"! He is always the same!

When I'm given a gift and truly it very well may be the gift of friendship and/or love, I thank that person 'a' giver but I also most assuredly thank 'the' Giver. Yep, I do. I also thank Him for the very circumstance of my life which enables me to receive from that one He's put in my path and nudged to give to me.

Let me say here that the 'gifts' haven't always been recognized as such initially but you know...I DO get it. Sometimes it just takes me a while. Most probably the same goes for you.

April 15

Sing to the Lord, all the earth;

Proclaim good tidings of His salvation from day to day.

Splendor and majesty are before Him,

Strength and joy are in His place.

1 Chronicles 16:23, 27

You know the earth does sing! Have you ever listened to the rain falling or the crescendo of thunder booming its voice to the heavens? One of my favorite things in all the world is to listen to the never-ending waves of the sea, splashing their song to declare the glory of God in His creation to those who listen. Glad tidings indeed are those which proclaim His majesty! Strength and joy are ever in His place and it is a place where each of us is welcome!

April 16

Do not be afraid of sudden fear

Nor of the onslaught of the wicked when it comes;

For the Lord will be your confidence

And will keep your foot from being caught.

Proverbs 3:25-26

Fear for me is not being prepared. It is that sudden smack in the reality of my life which leaves me staggering, especially when it comes out of the proverbial blue. Gobsmacked I've heard it called. Fear also comes when I'm scared, afraid for someone I love. Here then is where faith must enter. The Lord IS MY CONFIDENCE! He WILL NOT ALLOW MY FOOT TO BE CAUGHT because it is He who keeps me on the path which is straight and true and clear. I can trust Him for those I hold dear too. Though I fall short, He does not, ever.

April 17

The Lord is the portion of my inheritance and my cup;

You support my lot.

The lines have fallen to me in pleasant places;

Indeed, my heritage is beautiful to me.

Psalm 16:5-6

My dear friend Dotty reminded me that my husband shared this Scripture with me at our marriage ceremony lo, these many years ago. He has and continues to support my lot.

I'm not always sure about the second verse though, or at least in the midst of a complaining mood I certainly don't make the declaration of it. Here again, comes the faith part. I'm reminded of Corrie Ten Boom who praised God for the fleas in the concentration camp because they kept the guards from finding her Bible. Pleasant places? The thing is....she believed that her heritage was beautiful. Now THAT is faith and it is the kind of faith we are each called to walk simply because it is true.

April 18

"Behold, as for the proud one, His soul is not right within him;

But the righteous will live by his faith.

Habakkuk 2:4

When I was a kid we used to call proud acting, 'stuck up.' It's when someone tries to make those around them seem smaller or of no account. Truly it turns out the other way around.

The literal translation of the last line is:

"But the righteous will live by his faithfulness."

It doesn't say "by faithfulness" The Scripture here makes it personal. We are to live by OUR faithfulness! It is through Him that we've obtained that righteousness which is ours to lay claim to and live by!

April 19

Humble yourselves in the presence of the Lord, and He will exalt you.

James 4:10

Here is another 'thought' that I've used just once. It isn't a very pleasant nor popular one to be sure. Sometimes when I'm praying or in the 'Presence' of the Lord, I use my big boy voice and my big boy thoughts. It's just me and Him having a 'talk.' There are sometimes though, when I in my need, cry out to Him. It is those times when all the wordiness, all the saying the right things, is gone. Most often I'm letting Him know that I can't do it without Him and that is difficult for me. He gets ME. It is those times I believe this 'thought' is speaking of.

BTW, exalt means: "to raise in rank, honor, power, character, quality, etc.; elevate"

I'm pretty sure it is our prayers, our seeking His face He gives power to. He elevates, raises in honor those things that are His business and you know, that's us!

April 20

My flesh and my heart may fail, But God is the strength of my heart and my portion forever.

But as for me, the nearness of God is my good; I have made the Lord God my refuge, That I may tell of all Your works.

Psalm 73:26, 28

The last time I used this 'thought was in 1991 and then just the once. I'm wondering why?

You see, there is this place that I go when I'm tired, and when I'm not, when I'm angry and when I'm not. I go there when I need an ear to listen; someone whose agenda is to seek out the best of me. It is my safe place where my good friend can take all that I dish out and give me in return, always good, always clean and clear and honest. It is that place where Jesus Christ lives and it is the place where I am at peace. You have the same place.

April 21

The Light shines in the darkness, and the darkness did not comprehend it.

There was the true Light which, coming into the world, enlightens every man.

John 1:5, 9

In verse five the literal word for 'comprehend' is 'overpower.' It makes a difference to me. Comprehend means to understand and I don't believe that's the meaning here. Overpower means to conquer or defeat and let me tell you, the darkness DID NOT overpower the light!

There are seemingly two tenses used in verse five. "The light shines in the darkness" is now, it is continual. The second part of the verse says, "...and the darkness did not overpower it." It didn't overpower it past tense. It is FOREVER!

Ninth verse, same thing. There was....which does! There was the true Light which coming to us, DOES FOREVER enlighten every man because HE is FOREVER!

We will NEVER be in the darkness! The Word says that EVERYONE is illuminated, taught, has their path made light, through HIM!

April 22

For as the earth brings forth its sprouts,

And as a garden causes the things sown in it to spring up,

So the Lord God will cause righteousness and praise

To spring up before all the nations.

Isaiah 61:11

When I was a very little girl, there was a patch of grass on the other side of the fence, at the end of our yard. The grass there was a bit longer than our mowed yard and it was just grass, not like the weed-filled lawn on our side of the fence. It was wonderful to my little eyes. I remember always wanting to go there. At that same time, I also remember laying on the linoleum floor in our kitchen in front of the screen door thinking; "I have to get out of here." I must have been five years old.

What's the association here? Well, God gave me that little patch of grass. I know it. In the midst of the terrible turmoil I was living in, even then, He provided me with a place where "the earth brings forth its sprouts." His promise encompassed not only that little girl, it included and still does; every nation, every place. Where there is man, there righteousness and praise will spring up.

April 23

He who separates himself seeks *his own* desire,

He quarrels against all sound wisdom.

Proverbs 18:1

Have you ever been speaking with someone who isn't listening; who simply is waiting until they may speak to get their opinion/point across? This sort of response locks up a person's soul....not allowing them to escape beyond the borders of their own mind. The thing is...it also causes one to be alone, companionless, not letting the wisdom of God enter into one's life through those very ones God would seek to use to speak. There is a selfishness here whose outcome is never good.

There is too, a separateness which is quietness before the Lord. It is a listening before one speaks. This one brings life and wisdom.

My comfort zone is to be alone. When I'm alone I don't disappoint anyone, I don't anger anyone and I get my own way. Yep, in many ways it is selfishness. The question though is; what am I building? God's desire for you and me isn't to quarrel nor break out but rather to be/built together for His kingdom! In Christian lingo, it's called 'Building the Body of Christ.' Now THAT is worth not being alone for!

April 24

For judgment *will be* merciless to one who has shown no mercy; mercy triumphs over judgment.

James 2:13

A friend of mine wrote something on social media which I truly admired. It was a good, clean word meant to build up and not tear down in the midst of troubles besetting our nation. It was misconstrued by a shirt-tail acquaintance who really criticized it, using the most vulgar terminology. Well, there is a lesson to be learned here and I'd like to tell you I came up with it myself but I didn't. It came from a truly kind, wonderful fellow whom I've had the pleasure of knowing for many years. He shared a few words followed by the second part of the above Scripture; "mercy triumphs over judgment." ....and you know, it does, always.

April 25

Set a guard, O Lord, over my mouth;

Keep watch over the door of my lips.

Psalm 141:3

I was just talking with someone the other evening about praying after dinner when the day is almost done. In the morning there is hope for a good day, work to be done and positive things to look forward to. By evening at times those hopes have been dashed, what one has wanted to accomplish hasn't gotten done and there often seems to be a kind of malaise that has set in. This 'thought' speaks to that. Let my disappointed prayer be counted as incense. Let the lifting of my hands truly be an evening offering when I'm tired and life in general, seems to be difficult. Yes, in the evening, in the shadow of the day, oh God set a guard over my mouth and please Lord Jesus, keep a watch over the doors of my lips. Morning prayers are hope. Evening prayers are faith!

April 26

The lips of the righteous know what is acceptable,

But the mouth of the wicked, what is perverted.

Proverbs 10:32

I think we all know what movie/TV ratings are. R is restricted, PG is parental guidance, G is good, etc. One of the sons (I won't mention Brennan's name) when speaking about a movie or show will say, "It isn't rated 'Brennan.' I appreciate that. We as those ones who call on the Name of the Lord SHOULD know what is acceptable and have the boldness to make declaration of it! In a perverted world, it is important to speak out what is acceptable, what is righteous and what isn't! AMEN!

April 27

When I was a little girl, we had bedding at our house but certainly never matching. I remember seeing it at someone's home and wishing in my little heart that I could have it. Flash forward. When the sons were growing up, even in the 'sparse' times, I made sure they had matching bedding....duvet covers, sheets, pillowcases...you get the idea. Why mention this? Well, today you get the why first and then the 'thought.' When I received Jesus as my Savior one of the things He spoke to me was that He would give me "beauty for ashes, the oil of gladness instead of mourning," and "the mantle of praise instead of the spirit of heaviness." For me, that meant matching bedding. Such a small thing but when I add it to all of the small things, without number, it equals salvation, my having sons of righteousness, and my being planted firmly in Him so that He may be glorified.

It is just good to speak these words, knowing that they are true, knowing that He IS Most High over all the earth. I know you know it too!

The Spirit of the Lord God is upon me, because the Lord has anointed me to bring good news to the afflicted; He has sent me to bind up the brokenhearted, to proclaim liberty to captives and freedom to prisoners; to proclaim the favorable year of the Lord and the day of vengeance of our God; to comfort all who mourn, to grant those who mourn *in* Zion, giving them a garland instead of ashes, The oil of gladness instead of mourning, the mantle of praise instead of a spirit of fainting. So they will be called oaks of righteousness, The planting of the Lord, that He may be glorified.

Isaiah 61:1-3

April 28

If we confess our sins, He is faithful and righteous to forgive us our sins and to cleanse us from all unrighteousness.

1 John 1:9

It doesn't say; "If we excuse our sins."

It reminds me of when I hear 'but.'

"I'm sorry but...."

"I didn't mean to but..."

"I meant to do it but..."

"I shouldn't have done it but..."

Being real and in-person is standing up for who one is. When working with students during the past years, if they'd lied (and most had), one of the first things I did was to call them a liar. I would then go on to explain one should expect to be known by what one does, by who one is. If one lies, well then, one is a liar. If one works, well then one is a worker. They got the drift pretty quickly.

We are to confess our sins. "Yep, that's me. I did it." or "I meant it." God says when we do that He is there to forgive. The thing about forgiveness is that it also cleans. It's like washing with a bleach solution. Sometimes it stings and It sure isn't pleasant to experience, but the result is a wonderfully clean garment, fresh smelling and white. The laundryman is ever ready to do the wash too.

April 29

Do not let kindness and truth leave you;

Bind them around your neck,

Write them on the tablet of your heart.

So you will find favor and good repute

In the sight of God and man.

Proverbs 3:3-4

Kindness and truth are those fluttery butterflies; so beautiful to look at and so easily scared away. I must keep them though, as my constant companions. They carry their own fragile beauty with them and truly are a wonder to behold.

To find and to keep them most certainly brings favor and good repute in both the sight of God and of man.

April 30

And they sang a new song, saying,

"Worthy are You to take the book and to break its seals; for You were slain, and purchased for God with Your blood *men* from every tribe and tongue and people and nation.

"You have made them *to be* a kingdom and priests to our God; and they will reign upon the earth."

Revelation 5:9-10

I've always loved Revelation as I've loved the book of John and his perspective, his 'take' on Jesus. It is not that I understand all of Revelation because I most certainly don't. I do understand though, that it speaks of the culmination, the triumph of Jesus Christ.

You would be hard-pressed to find someone more patriotic than I am and yet, there is a kingdom that supersedes the kingdom of America. It is the Kingdom made by God for Jesus Christ and it is eternal. It is where we are called to be priests, where we shall reign on the earth because He said it! What a call to and a recognition of the Lordship of the Lion of Judah!

May

May 01

For I am confident of this very thing, that He who began a good work in you will perfect it until the day of Christ Jesus.

Philippians 1:6

......He who has the seven Spirits of God and the seven stars, says this: 'I know your deeds, that you have a name that you are alive, but you are dead. Wake up, and strengthen the things that remain, which were about to die; for I have not found your deeds completed in the sight of My God.

Revelation 3:1-2

Why these two verses? Both are perspectives on getting the job done, finishing what has been set before you to do. Cleaning up your mess. Note: Revelation doesn't speak of someone taking the burden, finishing the job set before YOU. It's a responsibility thing. It's also a principle. Be faithful in the small and you get the big. People who don't finish the small for the most part are never satisfied and blame others for why they don't have the big. We have God's Word which declares that "He who BEGAN a good work in you WILL perfect it." He will finish HIS job! He'll complete the task! He will get the job done! So must you and I!

May 02

This I recall to my mind,

Therefore I have hope.

The Lord's lovingkindnesses indeed never cease,

For His compassions never fail.

They are new every morning;

Great is Your faithfulness.

Lamentations 3:21-23

I do not serve a stingy God and neither do you! The word 'lovingkindness' is defined as tender kindness motivated by expressing affection and for 'compassion' a feeling of deep sympathy and sorrow for another who is stricken by misfortune, accompanied by a strong desire to alleviate the suffering.

God is often portrayed in the world as a stern taskmaster. Here is another picture of His character and it is a good one. When I am in the midst of it, this is He whom I turn to and He is ever there. He's there for you too

May 03

When my anxious thoughts multiply within me, Your consolations delight my soul.

Psalm 94:19

I used to drive a car with a manual transmission. That meant that I was more actively involved in going forward and backward, much more than driving a car with an automatic transmission. I had to DO something to make the car keep moving. I like that. This 'thought' reminds me of that. Sometimes I have to actively hand over my anxious thoughts to God. When I don't, they multiply and pretty soon I have a hard time getting where I need to go. That is when I literally give them to Him to carry, destroy or whatever HE wants to do with them. When I do that, He DOES delight my soul! He DOES comfort me and He gives me perspective! I get where I need to go without wrecking the car too.

May 04

As for you, the anointing which you received from Him abides in you, and you have no need for anyone to teach you; but as His anointing teaches you about all things, and is true and is not a lie, and just as it has taught you, you abide in Him.

1 John 2:27

I haven't typically liked this verse because at first glance it seems to say that we have no need for teaching. What it's saying though is pertaining to the anointing. There actually can't be any teaching, any word nor any outside input that supersedes the anointing we receive from God, as the anointing is literally the Spirit of God Himself! It is TRUE, it is not a lie and It has taught us to abide in Him! The last part is literally a strong command which most translations don't show. It says with strong emphasis, "...just as it has been taught you, ABIDE IN HIM."

Yep, I get it. So do you, methinks.

May 05

Then Asa called to the Lord his God and said, "Lord, there is no one besides You to help *in the battle* between the powerful and those who have no strength; so help us, O Lord our God, for we trust in You, and in Your name have come against this multitude. O Lord, You are our God; let not man prevail against You." So the Lord routed the Ethiopians before Asa and before Judah, and the Ethiopians fled.

2 Chronicles 14:11-12

Note here that Asa didn't say: "You are our God; let not man prevail against us." Asa understood that the battle was God's, not his. So often I take it upon myself to fight God's battles. It is here that I need to recognize that these battles are HIS. It is against HIM that hell will not prevail. Asa put the battle squarely where it belonged, this in the midst of his having 580,000 against the Ethiopians' 1 million men! May we both, you and I, ever understand that the battles so often claimed for ourselves, are HIS battles!

May 06

Praise the Lord!

Praise the Lord, O my soul!

I will praise the Lord while I live;

I will sing praises to my God while I have my being.

The Lord will reign forever,

Your God, O Zion, to all generations.

Praise the Lord!

Psalm 146:1-2, 10

I've used this "thought" just once. The literal translation of both the 1st line in vs. 1 and the last line in vs 10 is: Hallelujah! God!

Yep! It is good to "Hallelujah" God! He WILL reign forever, to EVERY SINGLE generation! Hallelujah indeed!

May 07

Teach me Your way, O Lord;

I will walk in Your truth;

Unite my heart to fear Your name.

Psalm 86:11

One translation of this (NIV) verse says; Give me an undivided heart to fear Your Name. I like that! So often my flesh is at war with (His) Spirit within me. The battle cry needs to be sounded and a declaration made! Teach me Your way, O Lord and I WILL walk in Your truth!

May 08

I also say to you that you are Peter, and upon this rock I will build My church; and the gates of Hades will not overpower it.

Matthew 16:18

The gates of hell lead to death. Gates are guarded for a purpose. Jesus Christ descended through the gates of hell and came back victorious. He brought with Him the authority to proclaim that those gates would not hold back, overpower nor stop His church from being built. It's like telling soldiers that the battle they are supposed to fight has already been won. It's the same today as it was then. We WIN!

May 09

He who rebukes a man will afterward find more favor

Than he who flatters with the tongue.

Proverbs 28:23

Where I come from, we call 'flattering' sucking up. I've done it and truth be told, most likely so have you. To be fair to me, I've flattered more than a few that I thought I'd better say something good about first so that I wouldn't say something bad. I guess it has worked for me but not sure for them.

To rebuke means to express disapproval. There is nothing wrong with showing/speaking disapproval. After all, it's how we correct our children and it's how our heavenly Father corrects us. It's the Spirit in which we do it that counts (and I do mean Spirit with a capital 'S'). That form of rebuke brings forth good fruit which of course is later ripe for the picking and good to eat. It reproduces itself too.

May 10

For I am not ashamed of the gospel, for it is the power of God for salvation to everyone who believes, to the Jew first and also to the Greek. For in it the righteousness of God is revealed from faith to faith; as it is written, "BUT THE RIGHTEOUS MAN SHALL LIVE BY FAITH."

Romans 1:16-17

I am convinced that in our relentless and unstoppable drive to give our offspring all of those things we either haven't been given ourselves or that we deem now essential for their very livelihood, we have taken from them the opportunity to hunger for a God whose provision is far beyond what we can hope for or imagine. May He in His wisdom, provide opportunity for them to experience that hunger, that walking by faith which is only filled by Him.

The Gospel is the POWER OF GOD! In IT the power of God is revealed by faith to faith! It's what we live by folks!

May 11

Like one who takes a dog by the ears Is he who passes by *and* meddles with strife not belonging to him.

Proverbs 26:17

What an apt Scripture. Have you ever taken a dog by the ears? I have. The only and instantaneous thing they do is to try and make you let go, which usually involves biting. When I attempt to 'advise' one of the sons, invariably his response is; "Thanks but no thanks." We aren't too set on niceties at our house and I'm not sure he realizes his retort is a slam but he does get the point across.

It seems like Jesus is a bit more laid back in His response to our meddling in things that aren't our 'business' but the outcome is the same.

By the way, caring isn't sharing. Just because I'm privy to something doesn't mean that I have license to blab it all around. Just sayin.

May 12

From that time Jesus began to show His disciples that He must go to Jerusalem, and suffer many things from the elders and chief priests and scribes, and be killed, and be raised up on the third day. Peter took Him aside and began to rebuke Him, saying, "God forbid *it*, Lord! This shall never happen to You." But He turned and said to Peter, "Get behind Me, Satan! You are a stumbling block to Me; for you are not setting your mind on God's interests, but man's."

Matthew 16:21-23

What's interesting here is that Jesus didn't tell Peter to simply stop talking. He told him to get behind Him. He called Peter what he was....a stumbling block who was getting in the way of the will of God, focusing on what he, Peter wished for instead of what God's interests were. I cannot look in two directions at once. Neither can you dear friend. If we are to press on in the things of God (and we ARE), then we must look forward lest we become like Peter, looking to his own interests instead of those of God. The thing is, when we are able to do this and sometimes it takes just the simple act of obedience, God is there! He brings relief and joy and the Spirit of Life to take the place of what's been in the past!

Side note: The cross followed Jesus to the crucifixion, it didn't go before Him. He took hold of our past, swept it away, and turned it into our future!

May 13

Therefore I urge you, brethren, by the mercies of God, to present your bodies a living and holy sacrifice, acceptable to God, *which is* your spiritual service of worship. And do not be conformed to this world, but be transformed by the renewing of your mind, so that you may prove what the will of God is, that which is good and acceptable and perfect.

Romans 12:1-2

I really hate rhubarb. Every year I make a bunch into jam which I freely describe as into being 'guilted' into doing. Well, I've been wrong about that. This year I was given a BUSHEL BASKET, crammed full of the stuff and I've made 4 batches (tripled), baked 3 cakes and still have one more cake to go, to use the stuff. I seriously just don't like it. What does that have to do with this 'thought?'

We give Him our bodies so that we can approve what He's doing, that it is well-pleasing and perfect. Well, what about when it doesn't seem well-pleasing and perfect? That's when the "mercies of God" come in...that's when the faith to hand over our bodies to Him, comes in, when we by faith, approve (yes, we get to approve) what the will of God is for us, that it is indeed well-pleasing and perfect. That's when, by the renewing of our minds, we get to trust Him, and walk in His perfect will. I don't HAVE to use all of the rhubarb, I GET to do it. I get to tithe it too. An added bonus! YAY GOD!

May 14

I, John, am the one who heard and saw these things. And when I heard and saw, I fell down to worship at the feet of the angel who showed me these things. But he said to me, "Do not do that. I am a fellow servant of yours and of your brethren the prophets and of those who heed the words of this book. Worship God."

Revelation 22:8-9

Did you catch the order here? An angel of God tells a guy not to worship him because they're both servants. He likens himself to man when it comes to the power of God and this is he who has delivered one of the most powerful prophetic words in the history of the world. What does he say?

"Worship God."

Yep!

May 15

For our citizenship is in heaven, from which also we eagerly wait for a Savior, the Lord Jesus Christ; who will transform the body of our humble state into conformity with the body of His glory, by the exertion of the power that He has even to subject all things to Himself.

Philippians 3:20-21

Citizenship is pretty important to me. I could write a few chapters on why that's so but suffice it to say that I love my country and no matter what mess it's in nor in what state it finds itself, it is mine. I am a part of it and I respect that and it. I can't imagine doing anything or having anything happen which would cause me to leave it short of Jesus' return. As strongly as I feel about it, there is a citizenship that I hold yet more dear. It is to be part and parcel of the Kingdom of God. It is that place where my spirit, my life, and the lives of those I love is secure, knowing that there I am being conformed/shaped into a citizen of heaven, by His power. It is a marvelous thing, that transformation and there's room for all.

May 16

The way of the righteous one is smooth; O Upright One, make the path of the righteous level.

Isaiah 26:7

Many years ago in Northern Ireland, I took a coastal path that led to a rope bridge, similar to those one sees in old Tarzan movies. Somehow I knew I had to cross that bridge. It led to a tiny island where of course the only thing one could do was to go back the way one had come. I did it. I went across and was so frightened by the experience that once across, I literally laid flat on the ground shaking. I must have stayed there for an hour or so. The wind began to blow and I began to think I just would have to stay there. A guy come up to me and said I must come back over because they were going to be closing the bridge as it was getting too dangerous to cross. He said, "I will guide you back. Just look at me and walk forward." That is exactly what he did. He walked backward, holding onto the ropes on either side, softly coaching me on. I've never been more afraid in my life.

I've often remembered that experience when I sensed God directing me down a difficult path. In the midst of my fear, there is this trust, this knowing that my path is smooth because He is there making it that way. He always and forever does.

May 17

Listen, O my people, to my instruction;

Incline your ears to the words of my mouth.

That the generation to come might know, *even the children yet to be born,*

That they may arise and tell them to their children,

That they should put their confidence in God

And not forget the works of God

But keep His commandments...

Psalm 78:1, 6-7

I've been thinking a lot about 'generations' lately, why some do evil in the sight of God, some do good and some do good to the extent that they take down the 'high places' where God has not been recognized nor worshiped. It is the responsibility of every generation to impart that very thing, the instruction of God that we across the ages, are to put our confidence in HIM! 'Every generation' means me. I am to tell my children and my children's children to not forget the works of God, to keep His commandments and it is not enough to tell them. I must live it for them to see so that they won't forget. So must you dear reader. So must you.

143

May 18

By this you know the Spirit of God: every spirit that confesses that Jesus Christ has come in the flesh is from God; and every spirit that does not confess Jesus is not from God; this is the *spirit* of the antichrist, of which you have heard that it is coming, and now it is already in the world. You are from God, little children, and have overcome them; because greater is He who is in you than he who is in the world. They are from the world; therefore they speak *as* from the world, and the world listens to them. We are from God; he who knows God listens to us; he who is not from God does not listen to us. By this we know the spirit of truth and the spirit of error.

1 John 4:2-6

If this 'thought' was a school course and it had a name, it would be:

Discernment 101

This is a double-fold 'thought.' It describes for us how we are to tell who truly is listening to us and how we are to respond to those who recognize Jesus Christ as their Savior, when they speak. By this Godly listening and speaking, we know the spirit of truth and the spirit of error. This by the way, is not given as an excuse for judgment.

May 19

For you have need of endurance, so that when you have done the will of God, you may receive what was promised.

For yet in a very little while,

He who is coming will come, and will not delay.

But My righteous one shall live by faith;

And if he shrinks back,

My soul has no pleasure in him.

Hebrews 10:36-38

When I am sick, I have no choice but to endure, to walk out that uncomfortable, painful place and position I'm put in. Sometimes it's the same in the Spirit. I know where my hope is and I know that He who promised is faithful, that he doesn't waver. I have HIS WORD. I WILL receive the promise! I just need to walk it out! If I would be required to do that without having had experienced/called upon faith, I would have no stamina, no endurance to do it and I would shrink away from it. That is not God's heart for me and let me tell you, this is a race I need to win. So do you.

May 20

Therefore, He had to be made like His brethren in all things, so that He might become a merciful and faithful high priest in things pertaining to God, to make propitiation for the sins of the people. For since He Himself was tempted in that which He has suffered, He is able to come to the aid of those who are tempted.

Hebrews 2:17-18

I am always reticent to accept help unless I ask for it, which isn't very often. When I do ask, it is from someone I trust, someone who won't remind me of my shortcomings when they've seen me fail or not be able to accomplish what I've set out to do. I don't think it's a pride issue. I believe it's that I'm afraid of not being in control or rather, having to give the control to someone else. That's Jesus Christ in a nutshell. He had to give complete control to His Father, believing that He'd do what He said He would do. Jesus is the same for us. He is there to come to my aid and He has experience in 'IT', whatever 'IT' is. He even understands when I need help to believe Him, and there too, He comes to my aid! Same goes for you!

May 21

Therefore, brethren, since we have confidence to enter the holy place by the blood of Jesus, by a new and living way which He inaugurated for us through the veil, that is, His flesh, and since we have a great priest over the house of God, let us draw near with a sincere heart in full assurance of faith, having our hearts sprinkled clean from an evil conscience and our bodies washed with pure water. Let us hold fast the confession of our hope without wavering, for He who promised is faithful; and let us consider how to stimulate one another to love and good deeds, not forsaking our own assembling together, as is the habit of some, but encouraging one another; and all the more as you see the day drawing near.

Hebrews 10:19-25

When I was a little girl, I had to help do laundry. We didn't have water in the house so I had to carry it from the well. Four buckets to fill the reservoir in the cookstove, six or seven, again depending on how full I filled the bucket, for each of two rinse tubs and then the washing machine, which was a wringer type. I can't remember how many buckets went into it but it was a lot. Anyway, while I hated laundry day, I remember I loved the smell of the result. A clean smell unsurpassed for both its crispness and its blue sky aroma. To this day I have this thing about laundry. I hate dirty clothes and I don't mind the scrubbing. Why this story? Well, it's like Jesus washing me. He did it once for all. I go about my business getting soiled. It doesn't show too much at first but then you know, I get more and more dirty, when I don't read the Word, stay in conversation with Him, and just let Him CLEAN me anew! That's what this Scripture is all about for me.

May 22

I wait for the Lord, my soul does wait,

And in His word do I hope.

My soul waits for the Lord

More than the watchmen for the morning.

Indeed, more than the watchmen for the morning.

Psalm 130:5-6

I used to have to 'wait' for my husband on a Sunday morning as he leisurely drove us to church, taking his time because it was Sunday and Sunday was for rest. No hurrying. My blood pressure goes up just remembering it! I would hurry like crazy to get all five sons fed, dressed, and in the van so that we wouldn't be the LAST FAMILY to arrive. I would have to wait while he drove slowly. Arrggghhh! Sometimes that's how I feel when I'm waiting on God. He doesn't respond to pressure though, nor hollering or bickering. He holds steady until I get my perspective, my 'vantage point' corrected, and in the right place. I've truly never considered waiting upon God like the waiting one does when looking for that moment when the sun peeks its way over the horizon. I'm going to though. I hope you do too.

May 23

For not one of us lives for himself, and not one dies for himself; for if we live, we live for the Lord, and if we die, we die for the Lord; therefore whether we live or die, we are the Lord's. For this end Christ died and lived again that He might be Lord both of the dead and of the living.

Romans 14:7-9

I have a hard time sometimes wrapping my mind around this one. I've lived for my family, and I'd like to believe that I have and continue to live for God. That leaves out the dying part though.

As retirement approached, I tended to say; "it's time I live for myself now." NO! That is a lie from the pit! May it ever and always will be that I live for HIM, that I seek His face MORE, that it is HE whom my heart and my soul is set upon! Whether I live or whether I die, His eternal purposes will out. Not me but HE!

May 24

For we are a fragrance of Christ to God among those who are being saved and among those who are perishing; to the one an aroma from death to death, to the other an aroma from life to life. And who is adequate for these things? For we are not like many, peddling the word of God, but as from sincerity, but as from God, we speak in Christ in the sight of God.

2 Corinthians 2:15-17

I WANT to be a sweet aroma to God. It's not as difficult to do it among believers. It's more challenging though when around those that don't play by my rules or rather, should I say those rules that I perceive as 'kingdom' rules.

And yet, God Himself, through His Word, has declared that I am/we ARE adequate to be the very aroma of Christ! The Scripture says we speak in Christ IN THE SIGHT OF GOD! A pretty sobering thought to be before the Throne of Grace whilst in a world that is sniffing to get an idea of what we smell like.

This isn't a call to flowery, gooey speech folks, this is a call to speak holiness and truth in whatever we say. This is a call to have the strength to stand up under the accusation of stinking when the truth we speak causes those around us to reel away from us, from the smell of death which pierces their soul, hopefully reaching them with words that redeem and are life-changing. It's to have the understanding that to those who have ears to hear, those same words aren't spoken to be claimed as empty words of phony praise but are rather like the balm of Gilead, bringing life and bringing the reality of who Jesus Christ is.

May 25

You are my hiding place;

You preserve me from trouble;

You surround me with songs of deliverance. Selah.

Psalm 32:7

Ever tried to hide when someone is making noise right beside you? This is a different sort of hiding though. It's the kind when I'm licking my wounds or I don't wish to speak with anyone because if I do, I'll cry and give myself away. I also hide when I have work to do and I can't seem to concentrate enough to get it done. Here comes God along in the midst of it, SINGING. Stage change. I can't stay 'hurt' in the midst of being delivered, rescued. I can't stay angry either and believe me, I've given it my best shot. He hides me enough to preserve me, keep me from trouble, and then you know, He DELIVERS ME! What a God I serve. Same goes for you!

May 26

And let endurance have *its* perfect result, so that you may be perfect and complete, lacking in nothing.

James 1:4

The literal word here for 'endurance' is steadfastness. That's important. Steadfastness by definition is being faithful, finishing what one has begun. It means to be firm in purpose, strong in resolution.

I remember many years ago, just being bone weary by the evening time which was made up of dinner to prepare, music lessons to be completed (Suzuki method thank you), homework to be helped with, school lunches to prepare for the next day, clothing laid out and very often, bread to be made for the morning. One was used to it but what I remember and it's the same now btw, is that I did each task on a mental checklist, knowing that when the list was done, I would be done for the day, and then I would have a bit of time to myself. In other words, I had a goal and I didn't get my 'reward' until the goal(s) had been met. Those years were a good lesson to me in my walk with God. There is a strength, an endurance built up in the doing of life and it's the same with one's walk with Jesus Christ. He is looking for and helping us to complete, to finish the race SO THAT we lack in nothing. I need to add here that those years were the best. I loved that time and am so grateful for the opportunity He gave me to experience it. Pretty sure it's the same with you. Enjoying the forest for the trees.

May 27

Teach me good discernment and knowledge,

For I believe in Your commandments.

You are good and do good;

Teach me Your statutes.

May those who fear You see me and be glad,

Because I wait for Your word.

Psalm 119:66, 68, 74

This is a progression for me. I know myself. I don't always have good judgment, good discernment, and/or knowledge. One thing I have though which has stood me well is that I believe. It is God whom I've taken my stand with, make declaration of. I've bought Him, hook, line and sinker. I've drunk the kool-aid is one way I've heard it described. You see I KNOW that He is good. I KNOW that if I know His statutes and I do, it is because He has poured them into my heart. If those around me see anything of me, I hope it is Him. I hope it is that good, clean fear of God that He's given me to keep as my own. I do wait for His Word and it is ever and continually coming, like a stream of cold, clear water. Have a drink. Its cost is your life.

May 28

Then Elisha spoke to the woman whose son he had restored to life, saying, "Arise and go, you and your household, and stay wherever you can; for the Lord has called for a famine, and furthermore, it will come upon the land for seven years." So the woman arose and did according to the saying of the man of God, and she went with her household and dwelt in the land of the Philistines seven years. It came to pass, at the end of seven years, that the woman returned from the land of the Philistines; and she went to make an appeal to the king for her house and for her land. Then the king talked with Gehazi, the servant of the man of God, saying, "Tell me, please, all the great things Elisha has done." Now it happened, as he was telling the king how he had restored the dead to life, that there was the woman whose son he had restored to life, appealing to the king for her house and for her land. And Gehazi said, "My lord, O king, this is the woman, and this is her son whom Elisha restored to life." And when the king asked the woman, she told him. So the king appointed a certain officer for her, saying, "Restore all that was hers, and all the proceeds of the field from the day that she left the land until now."

2 Kings 8:1-6

Why the story of the Shunamite woman? Isn't it enough that she almost lost her son and had to leave her life for seven years? Couldn't God have provided for her at home, in the midst of the drought? Well, I don't always get to know why God does things the way He does. I do know though, that God is a 'restoration' God. In the midst of the drought, He takes me to a place where He can keep me. It might not be the place of my choosing but it's God's place for me until in His care for me, he restores my 'fields.' Some of the most beautiful places I've lived have been those where I would have chosen not to go. I've learned through it all; drink where He tells me to drink. Methinks it's the same for you.

154

May 29

For no man can lay a foundation other than the one which is laid, which is Jesus Christ.

1 Corinthians 3:11

I'm pretty careful about laying my foundations, or at least I think I am. When I get ready for work, the foundation has been laid the night before. When I get up and come downstairs in the morning, the cone and filter have been laid out with the coffee, sugar, a spoon to measure the coffee, and of course the teakettle my dear friend Jackie gave me. All is ready. The foundation has been laid. One would think my foundation in HIM would have been laid as carefully. One could imagine that when I get angry I could go to that foundation I think I've laid out, that place of faith where I can drink the 'coffee', where I can draw from the place where I've invited Him in, that place in me where HE is the foundation.

I don't always do that, go to that place. The more I've done it in my life though, the more familiar I am with and in THAT PLACE. The good news is, I don't have to rely on myself. I might think at times I've laid the foundation but as a matter of fact, HE LAID THE FOUNDATION and HE IS THE FOUNDATION! That is what I draw from! I'm going to enjoy my cup of coffee now.

May 30

Guard my soul and deliver me;

Do not let me be ashamed, for I take refuge in You.

Let integrity and uprightness preserve me,

For I wait for You.

Psalm 25:20-21

I almost left out verse 20 and yet it has been my unspoken prayer for most of my walk with God. I grew up with shame. Some of my earliest memories are of wishing I lived with my neighbor's family where I thought there wasn't any fighting, where there wouldn't need to be secrets kept. HE KNOWS ME. He has set me in a high place where shame can't cling to me nor wear me down. Since HE is the author and the finisher and since HE's the one that runs this rodeo, He's teaching me to walk with integrity and with uprightness and I'm grateful for the lessons! Pretty sure it's the same with you.

May 31

Hear my cry, O God;

Give heed to my prayer.

From the end of the earth I call to You when my heart is faint;

Lead me to the rock that is higher than I.

For You have heard my vows, oh God You have given *me* the inheritance of those who fear your name.

Psalm 61:1-2, 5

I love the Psalms. David is my hero of all of the people spoken of and referred to in the Bible. Notice here, he doesn't say: "Save me" nor "Keep me" or "Heal me". What he says is: "Lead me to the rock that is higher than I."

He's asking God to give him a perspective that will allow him to see, to keep his head above the water. A place where his feet are firmly planted. In the midst of the asking, he has the assurance that God has heard him and that God has made provision for him; the inheritance of those who fear His name and what a provision it is! David gets to spend eternity with those who have made this Rock their reality! You know you and I are part of that inheritance!

That's what I'm praying for you who read the Scriptures in this book....that God puts you in that higher place, that place where you can see what it is that God has for you. I'm praying that for me too.

June

June 01

Two are better than one because they have a good return for their labor. For if either of them falls (literally "if they fall"), the one will lift up his companion. But woe to the one who falls when there is not another to lift him up.

Ecclesiastes 4:9-10

So I have my 'peeps', both family and friends. There are those who if/when I fall, I can give a call to. I've been picked up, pushed up, given a kind word, and sometimes....given a not so kind word, which was exactly what I've needed....to make sure that I receive what's required and necessary. SOMETIMES I haven't even needed to call! It's called 'Body ministry' and it is good. Body ministry peeps 'have my back.' It's reciprocated too. The Kingdom of God is a grand place to be, isn't it? The Body of Christ in the flesh.

June 02

Then the Lord answered me and said,
"Record the vision
And inscribe *it* on tablets,
That the one who reads it may run.
"For the vision is yet for the appointed time.
It hastens toward the goal and it will not fail.
Though it tarries, wait for it;
For it will certainly come, it will not delay.
"Behold, as for the proud one,
His soul is not right within him;
But the righteous will live by his faith.

Habakkuk 2:2-4

Habakkuk was asking God why He was allowing judgment
to fall on His people by the Chaldeans. God's response was
the 'thought' for today.

We are called to live by our faithfulness. It was the same then
as it is now. The time of the vision is right now, today. Let me
say again; "We are called to live by our righteousness.

It doesn't say 'by faithfulness'
The Scripture here makes it personal.
We do indeed live by our faithfulness!
It is through Him that we've obtained our righteousness!

June 03

"You are the light of the world. A city set on a hill cannot be hidden; nor does *anyone* light a lamp and put it under a basket, but on the lampstand, and it gives light to all who are in the house.

Matthew 5:14-15

This 'thought' has been ringing in my ears lately. I've been thinking about that 'city set on a hill.' That is us, folks! A city in a location like that can be seen for miles and miles. The thing is, when one is in a city like that, the view is amazing. THAT should be what our light causes others to see, to be a part of. Up there one has a perspective unimaginable from any other location. The air is clean and the sun shines brighter and while there's fog in the valley, it doesn't approach the top of the 'hill'. Jesus Christ gives us that sort of perspective and that light. It is never feeble nor put out and gives light to ALL who open their eyes to see.

June 04

"The beginning of wisdom *is*: Acquire wisdom;

And with all your acquiring, get understanding.

Proverbs 4:7

I make Adirondack mirrors. In the doing of it, I use nails and refuse to use glue of any sort. There's a reason why. I know that glue may come undone, given too much humidity, pulling on the glued piece, etc. Bark that has been nailed into place won't move, ever, at all. It also won't curl nor lose its shape.

Wisdom is like that. I can obtain it and glue it in place but if I don't nail it down, really apply it and use it, what good does it do and how long will it last?

It is crucial to know what is right and that in the knowing, one uses good judgment as a call to action, as a clear pathway toward righteousness.

June 05

Then those who feared the Lord spoke to one another, and the Lord gave attention and heard it, and a book of remembrance was written before Him for those who fear the Lord and who esteem His Name. "They will be mine." says the Lord of hosts, "on the day that I prepare My own possession, and I will spare them as a man spares his own son who serves him." So you will again distinguish between the righteous and the wicked, between one who serves God and one who does not serve Him.

Malachi 3:16-18

My husband and I choose almost always, to hang around with people who love and serve God. Not to say that we haven't on occasion had those others to dinner or for a 'get together.' It's just not the same though as having fellowship, speaking with the saints of God. In reading today's 'thought' I realized that it is the 'speaking to one another,' that the Lord pays attention to, to the point that it literally gets our name written in the BOOK OF REMEMBRANCE! Can you imagine! We get the reward of eternal life for hanging with those who know who He is and who walk with Him! HALLELUJAH! Because we speak of Him, He has made declaration that we are His possession!

June 06

Every word of God is tested; He is a shield to those who take

refuge in Him.

Proverbs 30:5

A number of years ago I had to leave a place which I loved, it having been sold from beneath my feet so to speak. It was just devastating to me and at the time, I declared that I would never again go there, even for a visit because I knew it would be too painful for me. In the midst of it, I remember praying, "Not my will but your will." and I meant it. I have to say, it was bittersweet because it had been the first place where I'd felt I was 'home' in my entire life.

Flash forward. The result of having to leave that place has been more, both spiritually and financially than I could ever have hoped for or imagined. It is no wonder that this Scripture both describes the 'test' and the 'shield' in one thought, one representation of who He is. He can only be a shield to those who pick it up and use it.

June 07

You are my hiding place and my shield; I wait for Your word.

Psalm 119:114

This defines for me, every part of my life. There are times when I need to hide away, to secret myself so that I can shrink inward and no one will be the wiser. There are also times when I charge out, swinging for all I'm worth. In each of these circumstances, there is God. He knows. His provision for me is to cover me, tuck me away when I know, and when He knows I need it. When there is a battle to be fought, again there He is; a protection which may be worn in the midst of a crowd or when I am fighting an enemy which lives only in my thoughts. I love Him for who He is and I believe. So do you and yes, I wait always for His Word because it truly is a hiding place and a shield!

June 08

Jesus Christ *is* the same yesterday and today and forever.

Hebrews 13:8

I've experienced things which I've loved.... and which I am not able to replicate. They become lovely memories that seem to fade with time. Jesus Christ does not fade away nor dim, nor become unclear. His Word, and He, have the same power they've had from the foundation of the world and it is that power, which He has imparted to me! It is this sameness that calms my sea. It is this sameness that blows wind in my sails and sometimes, brings me to that place where I can think. This sameness is my rock that I can stand on and in fact, am anchored to.

When I am sick, He's the same. When I am worn out, He's the same. When I am alone and begin to wonder who hears my cries of distress, He's the same and He is present, always. He's the same when I shout Hallelujah too! He is HERE! Can you imagine? He's the same for you!

June 09

At night my soul longs for You,

Indeed, my spirit within me seeks You diligently;

For when the earth experiences Your judgments

The inhabitants of the world learn righteousness.

Isaiah 26:9

The word, 'accountability isn't my favorite to be sure because it seems like most folks use it as a means to control (me). I've given this 'thought' quite a bit of a think and I just can't find another word which fits.

How does one teach righteousness? What is God after here? Before Christ in my life, I did what I wanted, what felt good pretty much always. It became a comfortable rut to be in and frankly, I've been working the entirety of my Christian life to keep out of that rut, sometimes successfully and sometimes not so much. The dreaded word 'accountability' plays in here. He has kept it ever before my face and try as I might, I couldn't escape it nor where it has led me. I'm accountable to my husband, my children, those whom I've worked with, and most importantly, to God, the master of the universe. It's been at times a school of hard knocks because I'm often a slow learner when it's something I've wanted that God hasn't. On a world scale, teaching righteousness seems about the same. Rather than experiencing birth pangs, the world is experiencing judgments that lead to righteousness and it is HIS righteousness which means it is ever good.

June 10

.....The Lord is near. Be anxious for nothing, but in everything by prayer and supplication with thanksgiving let your requests be made known to God. And the peace of God which surpasses all comprehension will guard your hearts and your minds in Christ Jesus.

Philippians 4:5-7

It's the 'anxious' bit that for me is difficult. I looked up the word 'supplication' and it means to ask for, beg, petition, seek. I am so grateful to God that He actually wants me to ask of Him! He wants me to entreat Him and to humbly pray to Him, to let Him know my requests AND, I'm not to be anxious because in the asking, His peace guards my heart AND my mind!

A dear friend of mine wrote me a while back: "I am not in charge. Thank God." I couldn't have said it better myself!

June 11

A brother offended *is harder to be won* than a strong city,

And contentions are like the bars of a citadel.

Proverbs 18:19

I'm reading over this Scripture, wondering why the Holy Spirit nudged me to it....about the same time I find myself being annoyed at someone. To tell you the truth, carrying a chip on one's shoulder isn't pleasant and the longer carried, the heavier it gets.

My faith walk means that I get what HE gives me and it's ENOUGH! If I am offended, let it be in HIM because HE can handle it and HE will fix it, not if, but when I let Him!

What is one supposed to do with an offense anyway? Just punch someone a good one in the nose and shake hands? What one can do, okay, what 'I' CAN do is give it to Him to carry, or throw away or whatever He wants to do with it. Done. Same goes for you.

June 12

Therefore thus says the Lord God,

"Behold, I am laying in Zion a stone, a tested stone, a costly cornerstone *for* the foundation, firmly placed. He who believes *in it* will not be disturbed (literally 'in a hurry).

Isaiah 28:16

I found myself perturbed this morning as I read the Word....seeking and praying for the 'thought'....why is it taking SO LONG? I have SO MUCH TO DO! I WON'T GET IT ALL DONE! Chapter after chapter of judgments on places, seriously? Then I came to the 'thought' for today and I knew what the Holy Spirit was trying to tell me. There is this place, this foundation that we believe in. He who believes in it will NOT BE IN A HURRY! We will NOT be disturbed! We need to be there because it is HIS place!

A while back one of my sons (I won't mention Scooter's name) told me that he remembered me as often angry when he was growing up. In reflecting upon that I realized that the root of a good bit of the anger was 'hurrying.' Getting stuff done to be exact. When someone wasn't fast enough or didn't produce what I thought was 'adequate' I became annoyed. How shallow is that? God has NEVER been in a hurry for me to accomplish that which He's put before me to do. As a matter of fact, He's been miraculously patient. I believe in this cornerstone Isaiah spoke of. I believe it is the foundation stone of a place that is for me and for you. I'm not saying I will no longer be in a hurry nor that I won't get annoyed but I will say that because of His mercy to me, this 'hurrying' will no longer hold me in its clutches. You too?

170

June 13

As is Your name, O God,

So is Your praise to the ends of the earth;

Your right hand is full of righteousness.

Psalm 48:10

Giving praise and giving thanks isn't the same thing. I give thanks multiple times a day to God. Praise, on the other hand, isn't so often coming from my mouth. Praise is for who He is, not what He's done. Praise is the expressing of admiration, willingly offering words as an act of worship. Praise to God does indeed go up from the ends of the earth by those who recognize His righteousness. Praising Him whom we serve shall come more often from my mouth. I hope yours too.

June 14

The Lord preserves the simple;

I was brought low, and He saved me.

Return to your rest, O my soul,

For the Lord has dealt bountifully with you.

For You have rescued my soul from death,

My eyes from tears,

My feet from stumbling.

I shall walk before the Lord

In the land of the living.

Psalm 116:6-9

I tried my best to find another word/translation for the word "simple" in vs. 6. I looked in different translations, looked up the literal meaning. It means what it says. Simple. The Lord preserves the simple. I guess if King David called himself simple, I'm in good company. Just like David, He saved ME. He has given my soul rest and He has dealt bountifully with me. He has taken away my tears and keeps my feet from stumbling. He's promised that I shall walk before Him in the land of the living. You too! I guess being called simple isn't so bad after all.

June 15

But now, O Lord, You are our Father,

We are the clay, and You our potter;

And all of us are the work of Your hand.

Isaiah 64:8

I've never used this thought before, not in thirty-plus years. I haven't always been an easy pot to shape nor I suspect have you. I've felt the need to be reshaped at times and I can imagine Jesus has seen the need too. This illustration is particularly apt. The last thing to happen is the firing and whether it's simply to strengthen the pot or whether it's to both color and fire the pot, it isn't a pot until it's fired. Trust God. He knows what He's doing.

June 16

"Offer to God a sacrifice of thanksgiving

And pay your vows to the Most High;

Call upon Me in the day of trouble.

I shall rescue you, and you will honor Me."

Psalm 50:14-15

The order of this seemingly makes no sense. Why would I thank Him and pay vows to Him when I'm in trouble? Shouldn't it be the other way around? Don't I first call on Him in the day of trouble, let Him rescue me, and then give honor to Him, give Him a sacrifice of thanksgiving and pay my vows?

This is a trust issue and a "keeping track" issue. I praise Him and thank Him for EVERY SINGLE THING in my life and believe me, it is difficult at times to give this sacrifice of thanksgiving. The thing is, it's also spiritual money in the bank. I BELIEVE that He has my back, that He knows what He's doing, that it is a good order to things when I fulfill my vows to Him to love Him, serve Him, and be called one of His.....knowing that THEN comes the payback Knowing that He DOES rescue and He does honor me! Can you imagine? THAT is the money I want in my bank. Yours too!

June 17

One hand full of rest is better than two fists full of labor and striving after wind.

Ecclesiastes 4:6

I have to tell you....it is HARD to lay down labor! One busies oneself to find one's worth. Well, at least I do. I'm not speaking of the labor to support oneself. I'm talking about that desperate striving to find acceptance in the doing. It is a hole with no bottom. It is hard for me to not measure acceptance by my human perceptions of it. Jesus though, uses a different scale, one in which I measure up, always. It's called being in His rest. Same goes for you. Rest is defined as refreshing oneself, the relieving of weariness by the stopping of work. To be able to step into God's rest, even a bit, seems to be better than fretting away...pushing oneself with no promise of reaching the goal nor really being able to hold on to what the goal is. I lose sight of the fact that Jesus Christ is the goal and I don't have to push to get there nor fret because I haven't made it. The rest of it is just wood, hay, and stubble which wears one out.

Where my labor is, there is my heart. It should be the other way around. Where my heart is, there is my labor. Simply put, it needs to be to serve God in all that I put my hand to. Period. That is not wind. That is real and it is where there is rest.

June 18

A rebuke goes deeper into one who has understanding

Than a hundred blows into a fool.

Proverbs 17:10

The dictionary defines a rebuke as sharp, stern disapproval; reproof; reprimand.

I HATE being rebuked because it says to me that I'm wrong, and I HATE being wrong. It brings out insecurities! It also says to me that I'm not in control of whatever the issue is, that it either is something that I need to repent of or that I need to see the truth of, so I can see the mind of God in the thing. A friend of mine said it shouldn't be upsetting but relieving and cleansing to my soul to be corrected or rebuked. The Lord is stopping an error that could germinate in my heart and bear bitter fruit.

One of my sons describes this verse this way:

"I actually think about the proverbs and discipline when I'm having a bad day sometimes. I know it's kind of dumbing down God's Word, but when something goes really wrong in life I try to consider that God made or let it happen for a reason, and maybe to discipline me. Trials and tribulations sharpen us and make us better if we have the right attitude, and sometimes I think God is simply giving us a nice slap on the butt. It's like Papa says, 'God punishes the small sins right away.'

Lol, I love that."

I couldn't agree more.

June 19

And He will judge the world in righteousness;
He will execute judgment for the peoples with equity.
The Lord also will be a stronghold for the oppressed,
A stronghold in times of trouble;
And those who know Your name will put their trust in You,
For You, O Lord, have not forsaken those who seek You.

Psalm 9:8-10

He's never said we wouldn't have troubles. As a matter of fact, He knows them before we have them. What He says is, He's a stronghold for us when we ARE in trouble.

A while back I was working with two students and one of them mentioned something about God. The other boy, a good friend of his, said: "I don't believe in God."

My response to them both was this (which I'm allowed to answer because they asked me!):

A policeman stops you because you are speeding and you tell him you don't believe in both the police and most certainly the authority of the ticket. You still get the ticket and you still have to pay the fine.

That's how God is. There comes a day when every man has to pay for the ticket OR someone else pays it for him. I'm glad God's got my ticket in His pocket and it's stamped, "PAID IN FULL."

So is yours.

June 20

Your God has commanded your strength;

Show Yourself strong,

O God, who have acted upon our behalf.

O God, You are awesome from Your sanctuary,

The God of Israel Himself gives strength and power to His people.

Blessed be God!

Psalm 68:28, 35

Another translation reads:

Thy God hath commanded thy strength:

Strengthen, O God, that which thou hast wrought for us

He commands the very strength and power He's given each of us. His desire for me is to show Himself strong on my behalf! I must let Him, give Him the 'go ahead' to do it. So must you! The power of God! Can you imagine?

June 21

Even to your old age I will be the same,

And even to your graying years I will bear you!

I have done it, and I will carry you;

And I will bear you and I will deliver you.

"Remember the former things long past,

For I am God, and there is no other.

I am God, and there is no one like Me.

Declaring the end from the beginning,

And from ancient times things which have not been done,

Saying, 'My purpose will be established,

And I will accomplish all My good pleasure'.

Isaiah 46:4, 9-10

I so often get caught up in the petty little annoyances of life....
they creep into my prayer life, my family life my work life...
I lose sight of the end game.

It's Him. The end game is Him. He continues to carry me, He
will deliver me and He will establish His purpose and
accomplish His good pleasure. It is indeed, all Him.

June 22

Truth (literally "faithfulness") springs from the earth,

and righteousness looks down from heaven.

Indeed, the Lord will give what is good,

and our land will yield its produce.

Righteousness will go before Him

and will make His footsteps into a way.

Psalm 85:11-13

I had this 'thought' almost exactly a year ago.
HIS faithfulness DOES spring from the earth!
His righteousness DOES look down from heaven!
Let me declare today that what He gives is GOOD!
Our land WILL give its produce to us!
....and of course,
His righteousness DOES go before Him and
it DOES make His footsteps into OUR way,
because He IS the WAY!

June 23

Though the fig tree should not blossom
And there be no fruit on the vines,
Though the yield of the olive should fail
And the fields produce no food,
Though the flock should be cut off from the fold
And there be no cattle in the stalls,
Yet I will exult in the Lord,
I will rejoice in the God of my salvation.
The Lord God is my strength,
And He has made my feet like hinds' feet,
And makes me walk on my high places.

Habakkuk 3:17-19

Habakkuk's people were facing the judgment of God as he prayed this prayer. They weren't in a 'happy' place. He puts it all in perspective. He's describing everything in the natural being stripped away...and YET, he can say, "I will EXULT in the LORD! I will REJOICE in the God of my salvation!

....because he knew and folks, we know too, that the Lord God is our strength! He makes our feet like hinds' feet so that we can walk on OUR high places! Do you see? Habakkuk is declaring that God has given him the strength to walk on HIS, Habakkuk's high places! What's the high place God has given you the strength to walk on? I stand with you to EXULT in the Lord and to REJOICE in the God of our salvation BECAUSE He has been and will always be our strength!

June 24

If we live by the Spirit, let us also walk by the Spirit.

Galatians 5:25

One would think this is a "slam dunk". In the natural, I say I accept or I 'follow' the law. For example, I accept the laws pertaining to speeding. Do I literally follow them? Not always.

In spiritual things, I recognize and accept those things spoken to me in the Bible. How do I follow them? It's by the faith in what I've heard, it's by His voice speaking to me and sometimes it's by His having to 'give me a ticket' because that's the only way I'll listen. it is by the very essence of who He is to me that enables me to 'WALK' by His Spirit, to FOLLOW Him who's called me! I'm okay with that and so is He.

In other words, I practice what He preaches. You too.

June 25

Do you not know that you are a temple of God and that the Spirit of God dwells in you? If any man destroys the temple of God, God will destroy him, for the temple of God is holy, and that is what you are."

1 Corinthians 3:16-17

The dictionary defines 'temple' as "a place where God dwells." A place one can come to take refuge, to be safe, where one is immune from being arrested, where one may seek asylum. As I was mulling over you, my "peeps" this morning I realized that yes, each of you in his/her own way is a sanctuary. Christ in you makes you a walking 'Holy of Holies.' You are also a place where people can come to seek a refuge, where people can come who need that place where they are simply 'safe.' Jesus Christ in you, has made you that place! I'm so grateful we're together in the same place!

June 26

So, as those who have been chosen of God, holy and beloved, put on a heart of compassion, kindness, humility, gentleness and patience; bearing with one another, and forgiving each other, whoever has a complaint against anyone; just as the Lord forgave you, so also should you.

Colossians 3:12-13

This is pretty clear, right? It says to 'put on.' Well, sometimes I'm pretty sure I 'take it off' depending upon whom I'm around and what sort of mood I'm in. Here's the thing. I've been chosen by God and so have you. He's the qualifier, the enabler. In the midst of my unforgiveness, He's where I need to go to lay aside my affront, my anger. When mentally, I'm chastising someone for their having (often unknowingly) pulled my chain, He calms me and if I give Him enough time, shows me the error of MY WAY. He forgives me too, allowing me to see the value in it. What a God and what a lesson! Wondering if it's the same for you?

June 27

"I loathe my own life;

I will give full vent to my complaint;

I will speak in the bitterness of my soul.

I will say to God, 'Do not condemn me;

Let me know why You contend with me.

'You have granted me life and lovingkindness;

And Your care has preserved my spirit.

Job 10:1-2, 12

I really wanted to just use verse twelve but one needs to realize the context here. Job is undone. Why does God put him through what he's going through? God doesn't answer him YET. It isn't time. The heart of the matter and really the entire book of Job may be summed up in verse twelve, and Job, man of God that he is....gets it!

I find myself jealous of Job's relationship with God. To be able to say; "Your care has preserved my spirit." is such a wondrous thing! It portrays an intimacy with God, a truly knowing the God whom one serves and loves. Job had an understanding of sin too and knew that his was a blameless walk. He was clothed with confidence in the God who had shown him lovingkindness, even in the midst of his misery. Through Jesus Christ, I have that same blamelessness. I can approach the throne of Grace and yes, I too have been granted life and kindness and His care has preserved my spirit. Yours too!

June 28

Render to all what is due them: tax to whom tax is due; custom to whom custom; fear to whom fear; honor to whom honor.

Romans 13:7

While this seems pretty straightforward, I've had to give it some thought. If someone has hurt me, do I hurt them back? Do they deserve it? If they've slammed a door in my face do I do the same thing? How about if they've honored me but I detest the thought of honoring them back because they stand for everything which I don't? The tax one is pretty easy. Don't cheat. Pay up. Custom, yep I can do that and pretty much, fear too even though it's mighty uncomfortable at times. Honor seems to be for me at least, the tricky one.

In each of these examples I've mentioned 'I.' You know it isn't about me and 'me' isn't made reference to here. It's about the other fellow!

'Render....what is due them.' It is never about what they've given or not given to me personally. It's about what their 'due' is. It's God who keeps track of that, not me. He's better at it than I am anyway. He's better than you too.

June 29

The spirit of man is the lamp of the Lord,

Searching all the innermost parts of his being.

Proverbs 20:27

I've had this "thought" only one other time in these past many years. I've always looked at our being a 'lamp' as that light that shines outward, bringing light to others. This though refers to that light, that spirit within us which reveals to God exactly who we are. Notice here that THIS light doesn't refer to the Holy Spirit. It refers to our very own spirit, our life, and in this light, the very light of our life, we are revealed to God in order for Him to know us through and through. May I suggest it is our conscience, a light which God gives to every person, in order to reveal our innermost parts?

June 30

If it is disagreeable in your sight to serve the Lord, choose for yourselves today whom you will serve: whether the gods which your fathers served which were beyond the River, or the gods of the Amorites in whose land you are living; but as for me and my house, we will serve the Lord."

Joshua 24:15

Joshua in this passage was speaking to all of the tribes of Israel. To put it into context, the meaning of the word "Amorite" is 'mountain people, tall and impressive' inferring that the Amorite spirit is a spirit of self-exaltation, the Amorites being fame-seekers. Joshua made a declaration not only for himself but also for his entire house that they would serve God. Good call. Very good call. Those declarations are important in the kingdom of God. May it never be about who we are, but rather about who He is! Just sayin.....

July

July 01

For though the Lord is exalted,

Yet He regards the lowly,

But the haughty He knows from afar.

The Lord will accomplish what concerns me;

Your lovingkindness, O Lord, is everlasting;

Do not forsake the work of Your hands.

Psalm 138:6, 8

I was reminded yesterday that I can 'remind' the Lord. I can (and do) say to Him,

"Here's what it says in Your Word. What are You going to do about it?"

Today on behalf of each of us, I'm reminding Him. He said He WILL accomplish what concerns us. He SAID His lovingkindness is everlasting. He DOES NOT FORSAKE the work of His hands and He most assuredly KEEPS HIS WORD! It's money in the bank folks and He does pay up! Remember Lord!

July 02

The Lord is my light and my salvation;

Whom shall I fear?

The Lord is the defense of my life;

Whom shall I dread?

Wait for the Lord;

Be strong and let your heart take courage;

Yes, wait for the Lord.

Psalm 27:1, 14

Sue's translation:

He is my light, my salvation, and my refuge. I have nothing to fear nor dread. Waiting for HIM is more life-giving than rushing into unbelief and terror. In HIM I am strong because HE has given me the courage to wait for HIM.

It's all HIM folks, but you know, it's Him and Me too and that includes you!

July 03

For God has not called us for the purpose of impurity, but in (literally, "the state or sphere of) sanctification. So, he who rejects *this* is not rejecting man but the God who gives His Holy Spirit to you.

1 Thessalonians 4:7-8

I've only used this 'thought' one other time.

Impurity is defined as the state of being impure, often something that is or makes impure.

Sanctification, on the other hand, is defined as being set apart as sacred, to render legitimate, to entitle to reverence or respect, to make productive of or conducive to spiritual blessing.

Sue's translation:

God hasn't called us to sin and death. He's called us to light and life. We reject this and we reject Him. Period.

July 04

....My servants will be called by another name.
Because he who is blessed in the earth
Will be blessed by the God of truth;
And he who swears in the earth
Will swear by the God of truth;
Because the former troubles are forgotten,
And because they are hidden from My sight!

Isaiah 65:15-16

Did you get this?

It has stuck with me....because I couldn't wrap my mind around verse 15 that says; "My servants will be called by another name. What is that? I wanted to know what that name is! It can't be our name which is written in the Book of Life because THAT NAME never changes.

I believe it is a word spoken prophetically for the ages to come, and that it is we who recognize Jesus as our Redeemer, who indeed are called by another name which is "Christ" ians! That very Name makes reference to us as those who belong to Jesus Christ and literally are known by His name! When we take that Name, we take the only Name that matters: Christ.

Peter speaks of this in 1 Peter 4:16.

If you are reviled for the name of Christ, you are blessed, because the Spirit of glory and of God rests on you.

Christ: The Spirit of glory and of God resting upon us. AMEN!

July 05

The fear of the LORD *leads* to life,

So that one may sleep satisfied, untouched by evil.

Proverbs 19:23

I woke up from a nightmare this morning and while I make it a point to not allow myself to use these kinds of occurrences to dictate what the "thought" will be, today is an exception.

I was afraid this morning and I carried that fear with me on the way to work. There is a reason why the Scripture says: "The fear of the Lord leads to life so that one may sleep satisfied."

Sleep is a restorative, whether it's a little or a lot. It is that place where both our soul and our body gets to let their defenses down and just "be". It is that place where our body eases the worry lines from our brow so that through rest, we may gain strength. It is also that place where we are seemingly unguarded. Nope, not happening. Even in sleep, in Him, we are not vulnerable. It says in His Word that our fear, our reverence for Him while sleeping makes a way for us to be untouched by evil.

I'm claiming Godly, restful sleep for myself and so can you.

July 06

Fools mock at sin.

But among the upright there is good will.

Proverbs 14:9

Yesterday I had a discussion on and off, all day with a colleague who btw is a good friend, a Catholic. We were discussing the law vs. grace and it was (is) my belief that every person has within themselves a sense of right and wrong according to the law. There is that sense of 'guilt' which one either responds to in a positive way or in a negative way. If you don't have Jesus Christ to pay the price of your sins, then because the law is the law and the price must be paid, you have to pay the fine yourself. This is no small thing and it's no wonder that the Word calls mockers of guilt, fools!

We 'get it.' We understand that God, and the price He paid for our guilt, will not be mocked. WE THE UPRIGHT in God, are (HALLELUJAH!) among those who are recipients of the very favor of God Himself. Can you imagine?

July 07

He who is not with Me is against Me; and he who does not gather with Me scatters.

Luke 11:23

Have you ever tried to herd chickens? Well I have, and let me tell you, it's the worst. They scatter every which way with no sense of survival nor of anything else that I can tell. That's one reason why they're easily caught by a fox or a raccoon who makes short work of them.

Jesus didn't speak this to the gentiles. He spoke it to the religious people, the Pharisees. We, the people of God are supposed to get this, the more so because we KNOW HIM! Whether we 'gather' in worship, in giving, in hospitality, in speaking a word; it's all in gathering unto and for Him. It's being FOR Him!

July 08

Whatever you do, do your work heartily, as for the Lord rather than for men, knowing that from the Lord you will receive the reward of the inheritance. It is the Lord Christ whom you serve. Colossians 3:23-24

I was often expected to do a particularly unpleasant job and I really didn't want to do it. I was to gather eggs out of the hen's boxes, put them into a little pail, and bring them to the house. I couldn't have been more than five or six. I didn't like doing it because I was afraid I would get pecked by the mama hen or even worse, that there would be a snake in the box. Anyway, I remember standing by the cookstove (we heated and cooked with it, burning cobs to fire it....another unpleasant job I had to do by filling the 'cob box' every day) and complaining. My mom said, "Well somebody has to do it and you're somebody." That put an end to THAT discussion. It stood me in good stead though because well, you know, there are times when God and my mom have felt the same way. "Well, somebody has to do it!" I can do 'IT' with a crappy attitude or a good attitude. I can do a sloppy job or a good job but any way you look at it, I still have to do the job because I'm SOMEBODY. It works quite a bit better if one (me) does it heartily as unto God. I remember the eggs.

July 09

For you are my hope;

O Lord God, You are my confidence from my youth.

By You I have been sustained from my birth;

You are He who took me from my mother's womb;

My praise is continually of you.

Psalm 71:5-6

It used to be that I didn't have a hope. I will tell you plainly that I was not raised with God. He captured me as a twenty-two-year-old and not without a lot of kicking and screaming. When I stray mentally back to those earlier days, I find myself caught up short. There were so many times when while not knowing Him, He sustained me. He claimed me from my mother's womb and I am so grateful that I've been able to spare my own children the pain of hopelessness I grew up in and yep, I praise Him continually. It is a good thing to do.

July 10

Beloved, I pray that in all respects you may prosper and be in good health, just as your soul prospers.

Peace *be* to you. The friends greet you. Greet the friends by name.

3 John 2, 15

While John is directing this Scripture to Gaius, (whom he loves), as I was reading this morning, it dawned on me that there truly was and is a 'thought' here! John addresses Gaius by name, pointedly declaring words of prosperity, health and that his soul would prosper. He later speaks peace to him and that he (Gaius) is both greeted and should greet the friends by name. Hmmm.

This was initially written to those few hearty souls who have read my 'thought' for the day over the years. Today however, I am making that very same declaration to you! I am calling each of you and am praying that in all respects, you prosper, have good health and that your soul would prosper. I am speaking peace to you and I most certainly am greeting you! May I be so bold as to ask you to do the same to those that God has given you to call 'friend?'

July 11

Do not be deceived: "Bad company corrupts good morals."

1 Corinthians 15:33

I have used this 'thought' just once. When I first really gave it a think, I figured well, duhhh. It goes a bit deeper than that for me upon reflection. Jesus invited 'street people' to His banquet but He didn't live with them. He understood that they desperately needed what He had to offer. He didn't dummy it down either. The illustration of a light bulb fits here. It works wonderfully (let your light shine!) until it starts to dim. Oftentimes it gets dimmer and dimmer and then burns out. Our light is kept bright through the Blood of the Lamb, forgiveness, price paid. Sin tries to replace the light with darkness. It doesn't stop God. It stops us.

July 12

The toil of a fool *so* wearies him that he does not *even* know how to go to a city.

Ecclesiastes 10:15

When the sons were in the process of becoming men...and had taken upon themselves some of the most menial of jobs, I would often hear them talking about both the job they were doing and their co-workers. Their comments usually had to do with what they saw and heard as a sense of futility; men and women without the hope of a future, no yearning for what was to come. Many seemingly had become so dull in their perceptions that they had no purpose; they had no goal of getting on down the proverbial road. That isn't us folks.

1 Corinthians 15 says: ".....be steadfast, immovable, always abounding in the work of the Lord, knowing that your toil is not *in* vain in the Lord." This 'toil' does indeed, get us to a city and its Name is the City of God!

July 13

The Lord is my strength and song,

And He has become my salvation.

Psalm 118:14

I was saved toward the end of the true 'hippie' movement. There were still a few communes, back to the landers and such around. The place where God hid me away and the fellowship I attended sang lots of 'self-written' songs which my sons would probably find amusing. Most of the time they were played by the same person who'd 'written' the song and those folks would be in the back of the room, not the front. One was allowed to just start playing as God led them or one could request a song. There were no lists to be performed. While to this day, I appreciate that kind of worship when it can be found, and believe me, it's a rarity; the thing I appreciated the most is that those 'songs' were simply Scripture put to music. That constituted the 'writing.'

"Trust in the Lord with all thine heart, lean not to thine own understanding..." or "They that wait upon the Lord shall renew their strength" to quote a few, have stayed with me. I sing Scriptures every day and am so grateful for having learned them that way.

He is my ever present strength.

He puts a song in my heart

and to me and to you,

He has become our salvation.

202

July 14

Above all, keep fervent in your love for one another, because love covers a multitude of sins.

1 Peter 4:8

Have you ever had someone hurt you whom you've trusted? Of course, you have! It is painful, hurtful, and bitter to one's soul. It can truly only be canceled out by love, okay...maybe by 'like'. I wonder sometimes if hurt followed by forgiveness is a test which one must pass. I know people who carelessly throw hurt around like rotten fruit, never caring who it hits nor how much damage it causes. They are difficult to be around when the fruit is aimed at me.

I remember one occasion when my dear husband demanded that I forgive him. Of course, I was offended....until I thought it through. I do the same thing with Jesus and you know He always forgives me because of the love He has for me. He covers me in my sin and yep, I'm called to do the same thing. So are you.

July 15

For the churning of milk produces butter,

And pressing the nose brings forth blood;

So the churning of anger produces strife.

Proverbs 30:33

Anger is like a dry, old bone. One can chew on it to make it sort of worthwhile to keep on chewing, or so it seems....the fact is though, that it feeds no one and doesn't bring about life but rather, death...not because there is no sustenance in it but rather because it seems to be providing food when it isn't.

July 16

He who pursues righteousness and loyalty

Finds life, righteousness and honor.

Proverbs 21:21

What an odd Scripture. On the surface, I wouldn't have thought 'loyalty' would be included in this verse. It's defined as 'faithfulness and/or adherence to someone or something. It makes sense though. Jesus Christ being my pattern, is always righteous, always loyal.

Though one speaks ill of me, I am to be loyal. Though one ignores me or pushes me away, I am to be loyal. When one has hurt someone I love dearly, I am to be loyal, to both parties.

Here I must speak for clarity's sake. Sometimes being loyal is simply keeping my mouth shut. This for me is the most difficult. I can do it, no problem....if it involves covering someone's inadequacies. If they've hurt me or someone I love though...well, it is much more difficult. This is exactly when I need to walk in the strength of Jesus Christ, knowing that HIS loyalty covers a world of sinners, including me. He knows everyone's truths and it is He who defines who we are. True loyalty. What a pattern He's given us to follow!

July 17

'Do not fear, for I am with you; Do not anxiously look about you, for I am your God. I will strengthen you, surely I will help you, Surely I will uphold you with My righteous right hand.'

Isaiah 41:10

I grew up in fear and I can remember it vividly. It was one of the very first things Jesus dealt with when I allowed Him to come into my heart.

I no longer had to anxiously look about nor fret that somewhere, sometime, the proverbial ax would fall. He promised me is that HE will give me strength not from within me, but from Him. HE will help me, I don't have to try to figure out how to help myself because HE does it. HE'S got this! HE upholds me with HIS righteous right hand! You know He's kept His Word.

Pretty sure it's the same for you!

July 18

Though the wicked is shown favor, He does not learn righteousness,

He deals unjustly in the land of righteousness

And does not perceive the majesty of the Lord.

O Lord our God, other masters besides you have ruled us

But through You alone we confess your name.

Isaiah 26:10, 13

I am wrestling with these Scriptures! For me, they are about judgment and it's an eternal judgment I'm referring to here. God is an eternal score evener. He gave us free will and the earth as our footstool. He does not take back what He gives. How we use it is truly our choice. Otherwise, we would be puppets on a string. When we messed up, attempting to put ourselves on the same level as Him, He provided a way to fix it for us if we chose, through His Son.

The wicked ARE shown favor, as are those who call on the Name of Jesus. The wicked however do not learn righteousness. One can't use what one doesn't know. The essence of what ice cream is, cannot be described unless one has tasted it and experienced that it is good.

We know Him. We know that those 'other rulers' are faithless and do not seek our good, and this is the crux of the matter for me. I personally know that He seeks my good. I know it for you too. To confess His Name is what He is due.

July 19

Now may the Lord of peace Himself continually grant you peace in every circumstance. The Lord be with you all!

2 Thessalonians 3:16

I keep coming back to 'peace.' As I read a few definitions of the word, looking for seemingly the 'right' definition, I realized that the Lord is All of them! He is the Lord of every one of those definitions. HE can and does grant peace however one chooses to define it!

The literal translation of the word 'circumstance' is 'way.' The translated word 'circumstance' is here to limiting for me. 'Way' on the other hand is all-encompassing. It includes every method, every plan, and every means of getting where one goes. It also means at times to stand still and seemingly do nothing. That is a way too! The point here is that HIS WAY, the way He desires us to stand, walk, sit or be still, is the way of peace. It is the letting go of 'me' and the taking up of Him who IS the WAY! It is THAT PEACE which I hope for you too!

July 20

For *it is* time for judgment to begin with the household of God; and if *it begins* with us first, what *will be* the outcome for those who do not obey the gospel of God? And if it is with difficulty that the righteous is saved, what will become of the godless man and the sinner? Therefore, those also who suffer according to the will of God shall entrust their souls to a faithful Creator in doing what is right.

1 Peter 4:17-19

It is with difficulty that the righteous are saved? For myself, it's because faith is a fickle thing. How does one convince someone of the merit of believing when the Rock one stands on isn't always visible? In the midst of that there must be a judgment upon the house of God if it presents a soiled, tattered picture to a world that desperately needs Jesus Christ; He without spot or wrinkle. It is not given to me to understand the 'why' of suffering according to the will of God except to say that God knows the plan and I don't. He is faithful when at times I am not. He ALWAYS does right and I must give willingly, my soul to Him, my faithful Creator and yes, I must do right. Judgment must be shown as a witness to the world that there is order in His Kingdom. It truly must be; "Not me but He."

July 21

A fool does not delight in understanding, But only in revealing his own mind.

Proverbs 18:2

Have you ever been around someone that wasn't listening to what you were saying? They were just waiting politely (and sometimes not so politely) to be able to speak their own mind. Let me apply this to Jesus Christ. At times I sort of listen to that still, small voice but there are many times when I'm not paying attention, just biding my time until I can 'speak.' My hope for me, and you too, is that we don't delight in our own understanding. That we aren't so impatient, so narrow-minded that our only interest is in revealing our own mind to Him. To delight in what He reveals is ever so much more life-giving!

July 22

Finally, be strong in the Lord and in the strength of His might. Put on the full armor of God, so that you will be able to stand firm against the schemes of the devil.

Ephesians 6:10-11

Note: it doesn't say "try" to be strong in the Lord and in the strength of His might. BE STRONG! Put on the FULL armor of God!

Later in the chapter, Paul describes the armor:

Girding your loins with Truth

The Breastplate of Righteousness

Putting on your feet the preparation of the Gospel of Peace

The Shield of Faith

The Helmet of Salvation

The Sword of the Spirit which is the Word of God

PUT YOUR ARMOR ON! There is good reason to have it or He wouldn't have given it!

July 23

"I, wisdom, dwell with prudence,

And I find knowledge *and* discretion.

Proverbs 8:12

I had to look up the definition of 'prudence' to make sure I understood what the Word was saying.

By definition it is the quality or fact of being wise in practical affairs, as by providing for the future.

Sue's translation:

So be at the alert, ready for the future. Gain for yourself the ability to handle what comes your way and in the midst of that....know when to keep your mouth shut. Yep!

July 24

The Lord sustains all who fall

And raises up all who are bowed down.

The eyes of all look to You,

And You give them their food in due time.

Psalm 145:14-15

The older I get, the more difficult it is to 'get up' and the more I 'hunch over' as my dear husband says. Well, actually he says, "Ya, so you need to stand up, hey!"

He is correct. He would always help me if I asked but there's another one whose help is ever more ready to be asked for. It's that 'faith' thing again. God ALWAYS gives in due time, His time and it is exactly, squarely when needed; not a moment sooner nor a moment later. It's the leaning on Him which I have to get better at. Faith in action! You too methinks!

July 25

Your word I have treasured in my heart,

That I may not sin against You.

I shall delight in Your statutes;

I shall not forget Your word.

Psalm 119:11, 16

Most of the time, I treasure the words spoken/written to me both by my husband and my sons. When we disagree and after I've calmed down, I often remember their kind words to me, meant to build me up. They are my "go-to" place when it gets a bit rocky. I make the decision to 'delight myself' in those kind words they've sent me over the years and absolutely do not forget them.

It's the same with God who saved me, only more so. His WORD I continually choose to treasure in my heart. It is a balance, a check for me to not sin against Him. I make the decision to delight in His statutes and to not forget His Word to me. I do not take lightly nor minimize this treasure, this Word which He's given to me and I'm pretty sure you don't either.

July 26

Why are you in despair, O my soul?

And why are you disturbed within me?

Hope in God, for I shall again praise Him,

The help of my countenance and my God.

Psalm 43:5

Ever experience being 'bummed'? I call it 'doom and gloom.' I don't have to be going through earth-shattering experiences to have it plague me either.

I know better and so do you. There are times when I simply need to put on my 'big boy pants' and just get on with it. I know where my hope is and believe me, it isn't in my feelings. Always, there is a continuity with God, a walking in faith, a knowing that HE IS MY HELP. It is dangerous ground to give in to a bad mood. We know better, you and me.

July 27

"Behold, the days are coming, declares the Lord,

"When I will raise up for David a righteous Branch;

And He will reign as king and act wisely

And do justice and righteousness in the land.

"In His days Judah will be saved,

And Israel will dwell securely;

And this is His name by which He will be called,

'The Lord our righteousness.'

Jeremiah 23:5-6

Why this 'thought'? I was reading in Jeremiah this morning about God's judgment on an unbelieving generation. ....and then OHO! This prophetic Word of God which speaks of the Messiah, the Branch, in the midst of judgment shows itself! In an evil generation that does not seek nor listen to God, yet He makes declaration on our behalf!

The thing that stands out for me is that even then God names Him, declares that He is OUR righteousness! He speaks of Him not as His but rather as OURS! He is identified as the Lord OUR righteousness then and now!

We walk in OUR righteousness today. Every day is today!

July 28

Anyone who goes too far and does not abide in the teaching of Christ, does not have God; the one who abides in the teaching, he has both the Father and the Son.

2 John: 9

The literal translation here is interesting. It says, "Everyone who goes on ahead and does not abide in the teaching of Christ....." The big picture seems to be one's propensity to form new religiousness, new sects for lack of a better term, that do not adhere to the teachings of Christ. The personal picture though is simply going and getting ahead of where God has one to be. It's about waiting upon the Lord which of course once again is walking by faith with Him ever alongside.

July 29

Tremble, and do not sin;

Meditate in your heart upon your bed,

And be still. *Selah.*

Offer the sacrifices of righteousness,

And trust in the Lord.

Psalm 4:4-5

Once again, the literal translation here is important. The first line of this Psalm says this:

Tremble with fear or anger but do not sin;

Have you ever tried to be 'still' when you're in fear or angry? Especially when I go to bed, it seems that I must 'rehash' the day's seeming injustices, hurts to me and mine that have taken place. It is a sacrifice to switch gears, to go to that quiet place where I can meditate in my heart; to reach the point where I can be still. It is in the expectation of those moments that God calls me to trust in Him, to give my anger to Him. Pretty sure it's the same for you.

July 30

If you address as Father the One who impartially judges according to each one's work, conduct yourselves in fear during the time of your stay *on earth*; knowing that you were not redeemed with perishable things like silver or gold from your futile way of life inherited from your forefathers, but with precious blood, as of a lamb unblemished and spotless, *the blood* of Christ. For He was foreknown before the foundation of the world, but has appeared in these last times for the sake of you who through Him are believers in God, who raised Him from the dead and gave Him glory, so that your faith and hope are in God.

1 Peter 1:17-21

'IF' I call myself an adult, I am held accountable to act like one. 'IF' I address as Father the One who impartially judges according to each one's work, then I am accountable to conduct myself in fear, knowing by whose precious blood I was redeemed!

He has appeared for our sakes, yours and mine, having been raised from the dead and given glory by God so that we have a living hope. Jesus Christ is His Name. There is no better Name and truly, no better hope.

July 31

Then Hannah prayed and said,

"My heart exults in the LORD;

My horn is exalted in the LORD,

My mouth speaks boldly against my enemies,

Because I rejoice in Your salvation.

"There is no one Holy like the Lord,

Indeed, there is no one besides You,

Nor is there any rock like our God."

1 Samuel 2:1-2

Hannah is one of my faith heroes. Hers is a battle cry directed not to those around her but to Almighty God! Oh that this be on my own lips and on yours!

Dear God,

My heart does exalt in You;
My horn is exalted in You,
My mouth speaks boldly against my enemies,
Because I rejoice in Your salvation.
There is no one Holy like You,
Indeed, there is no one besides You,
Nor is there any rock like our God.

August

August 01

"Boast no more so very proudly,

Do not let arrogance come out of your mouth;

For the LORD is a God of knowledge,

And with Him actions are weighed.

"He keeps the feet of His godly ones,

But the wicked ones are silenced in darkness;

For not by might shall a man prevail.

1 Samuel 2:3, 9

Here is a continuation of yesterday, of Hannah's prayer. I have used this thought just once before, February 2nd, 2012. It is one of those 'favorite' Scriptures of mine. During all the years of child-rearing, I tried to be 'fair.' If I, for example, spent a certain amount on one child's birthday, I made sure I spent pretty much the same amount on each of the rest of them. Same for clothing, Christmas, etc. I'm still that way and tried to be fair as best I could with the myriad of students I worked with over the years, including the ones who were difficult.

Here is God's fairness. He knows my heart and He knows yours. I can't seem to be one way and then be another. He weighs my heart and has given me a promise with regard to it. It has never been about me or you either for that matter. "...not by might shall a man prevail."

August 02

Though all the peoples walk

Each in the name of his God,

As for us, we will dwell

In the name of the Lord our God forever and ever.

Micah 4:5

This is the Scripture God gave me for my wedding day as part of my vows to my husband. I meant it and it is for me a declaration of faith. It is important to stand, to 'live' for something. Some folks live for their jobs, some folks for their families. It isn't enough. Where we live is in the Name of the only Name and that Name is God and through His Son, Christ Jesus, by His Word, the Holy Spirit!

August 03

But you, beloved, building yourselves up on your most holy faith, praying in the Holy Spirit, keep yourselves in the love of God, waiting anxiously for the mercy of our Lord Jesus Christ to eternal life. And have mercy on some, who are doubting; save others, snatching them out of the fire; and on some have mercy with fear, hating even the garment polluted by the flesh.

Jude 20-23

I recently had a bit of a Facebook confrontation (and yes, I still do FB). Quite frankly, it took me aback. First of course came the righteous indignation. Next came the contemplation spiced of course with a bit of 'I want to get the sucker,'.... crush him with the Word.

My dear husband set me straight on the matter this morning. As we were praying together, he began beseeching the Lord on the fellow's behalf, asking for mercy for him. Boom! He is right on the money. I thank God for giving me a mate who ever has God before Him, who seeks His face on both my behalf and in this case, the fellow who castigated me.

An addendum needs to be added here and let me say that I appreciate how God works. As we were praying, I saw a picture of a guy decked out as a boxer, getting a short jab to the jaw. It was just one fast punch. Irrespective of me, my son had written a response to the fellow which was short and to the point. It was written as a correction and not as pain or vindictive hurt. Sometimes mercy and a short jab do just the trick.

224

August 04

God is Spirit, and those who worship Him must worship in spirit and truth.

John 4:24

I love this Word. It is black and white; no grey. If I'm playing baseball, I have to play by baseball rules, not soccer rules. I'm required to learn and understand the rules and use them, not because they are mean and worrisome but rather because it is what gives structure and life to the game. Walking with and worshipping God isn't a game but the rules apply nevertheless. If I am to worship Him (and I DO), I must do it in Spirit and in truth because it is what gives life. Period.

We as those who recognize Him as our God must worship Him in the Holy Spirit, in the form that He has given us here on earth as a helper and we must do it in truth....as an indisputable fact. Truth doesn't leave room for falsehood nor unbelief.

August 05

Let my meditation be pleasing to Him;

As for me, I shall be glad in the LORD.

Psalm 104:34

I've used this 'thought' just one other time and it was with another Scripture. Hmmm. It is one of those verses that I live in. How often during the day do my thoughts stray to what is unbelief or to what is unwholesome for me to dwell on...and then, MOST of the time I shake myself mentally and come back to that place....that place where what I'm dwelling on becomes a reflection of who Jesus Christ is in my life. It is exactly in that place where my heart is to be, the place where I meditate upon the truth that I am called to make the decision to be glad in the LORD. You too my friend, you too.

August 06

For if the blood of goats and bulls and the ashes of a heifer sprinkling those who have been defiled sanctify for the cleansing of the flesh, how much more will the blood of Christ, who through the eternal spirit offered Himself without blemish to God, cleanse your conscience from dead works to serve the living god?

Hebrews 9:13-14

I don't often think about the cleansing of my conscience. I almost skipped over that part while reading Hebrews this morning. I get that God, through the blood of animals set up the system for there to be a 'repayment' for the sins of the people and then in the New Testament, replacing the blood of animals with HIS blood as the payment for our sinning. I get all of that. Our God is a God though who not only covers our sins...He also cleanses our conscience from dead works. That is, He takes away the guilt of our putting our hand to things in the past that haven't been a part of Him...dead works. He restores a conscience deadened by what the world has to offer. Can you imagine? The end game here is so that we serve the Living God, and make no mistake; it is serving God that is the end game!

A dear friend reminded me, He also allows us to forgive ourselves by the cleansing. AMEN!

August 07

As for a rogue, his weapons are evil;

He devises wicked schemes

To destroy the afflicted with slander,

Even though the needy one speaks what is right.

But the noble man devises noble plans;

And by noble plans he stands.

Isaiah 32:7-8

Have you ever made a plan that you knew God's blessing rested on? I had only been a believer a few years; a baby Christian to be sure. I made no bones about a plan I'd made and I was brought before the elders because of it. One of them (my boss actually as I was the secretary of the church at that time) really let me have it. He didn't like 'my' plan. I sensed I was to be still, to not stand up for myself nor utter a word in my defense so that is what I did. Within a matter of minutes after his chastisement directed toward me, the other elders let him have it. They came to my defense with the matter ending with him apologizing to me and all of them praying for me! I wish every story of mine had that kind of ending but it fits the bill for illustrating this Scripture.

The dictionary defines 'noble' as, "admirable in dignity of conception, manner of expression, execution, or composition."

With Jesus Christ the author and finisher of our faith, the plans that we devise are good! We can stand on them just like we can stand on Him! Can you imagine?

August 08

"For as the rain and the snow come down from heaven,

And do not return there without watering the earth

And making it bear and sprout,

And furnishing seed to the sower and bread to the eater;

So will My word be which goes forth from My mouth;

It will not return to Me empty,

Without accomplishing what I desire,

And without succeeding *in the matter* for which I sent it.

Isaiah 55:10-11

One of the reasons I began the 'thought' was exactly because of this Scripture. "So will My word be which goes forth from My mouth; it will not return to Me empty, and without succeeding in the matter for which I sent it."

You know I believe that as much now as I did way back then, living in a log house in northern Minnesota. This gift, this wonderful living Word ever and always serves the purpose He intended for it.

It is the crux of every person's faith. To believe it is to truly trust God in whatever circumstance He has one in. To deny it is to live a life having never experienced His mercy and His grace. Either He is who He says He is or He isn't.

August 09

See how great a love the Father has bestowed on us, that we would be called children of God; and *such* we are. For this reason the world does not know us, because it did not know Him.

1 John 3:1

I hang out with the people I know because I can relate to them, I have things in common with them. When I meet someone new, it takes me a while to 'familiarize' myself with them. My husband says though, that I make up my mind pretty quickly as to whether I want to befriend them or not. That's probably true. In my defense, it seems that there is 'That' within me which reaches out to 'That' within them. Do I 'know' other people? Of course, I do and many I am ever so grateful for in my life.

It's been like that with Jesus and me too. I didn't know Him nor recognize Him until I was introduced and decided to 'befriend' Him. I'm not excusing, just explaining. This 'thought' gives me a whole new perspective on 'strangers.' I'm so grateful that HE knows each of us and it is through HIM, that we are Children of God with a capital 'C'! In Him we will never be strangers again.

August 10

"Behold, I am the Lord, the God of all flesh; is anything too difficult for Me?"

Jeremiah 32:27

I thought about explaining the context of this passage as I'm quoting it. I don't need to. This statement is true no matter how or where or when it's used and it is the crux of every person's faith. To believe it is to truly trust God in whatever circumstance He has one in. To deny it is to live a life having never experienced His mercy and His grace. Either He is who He says He is and He can do what He says He can do or He isn't and He can't.

August 11

For we have become partakers of Christ, if we hold fast the beginning of our assurance firm until the end...

Hebrews 3:14

A few years ago right before my retirement, I was at a 'behavior planning meeting' where all of the supports the school would provide in the upcoming year were being discussed, hashed over, etc....you get the drill. I left after ten minutes. In trying to wrap my head around the 'system' vs. what I'd done, I came to the realization that my time working as a behavior interventionist lo, these many years was NEVER about the system, not to say that I've ignored it....it's always been about God and me; about His leading and my following. It has been about the assurance that I've had since the moment I received Him into my life that HE would take me where I needed to go and HE would bring those ones to me that I needed to see. It is THAT ASSURANCE which I hold firm until the end. He leads you too, every single one of you...often not on the easy path but always, the path that leads directly to Him.

August 12

Praise the Lord, all nations;

Laud Him, all peoples!

For His lovingkindness is great toward us,

And the truth of the Lord is everlasting.

Praise the Lord!

Psalm 117

This is the very declaration that He is the God, the Lord of ALL nations!

We, the people of everywhere(!) are to extol, highly praise Him!

because....

His lovingkindness PREVAILS over us!

His faithfulness is EVERLASTING!

He WINS, which means that we win, always!

August 13

I have seen that nothing is better than that man should be happy in his activities, for that is his lot. For who will bring him to see what will occur after him?

Ecclesiastes 3:22

Sue's translation:

I have come to the realization that nothing is better than to make the decision to be happy in whatever I put my hand to, for this is what God has orchestrated for me to do. It has not been given to me to see the future.

What an awesome Word to live by, continually making a decision to walk in happiness, which is medicine for my soul!

As I was reading Ecclesiastes this morning, I found myself to be rather annoyed. Seriously....how could Solomon be so wise and be such a whiner and fatalistic? "Poor me, I have everything the world has to offer, I've done it all and seen it all and it's all for nothing." Really? At least in the midst of his misery, there is a ray of light! He does come to the conclusion that MAN SHOULD BE HAPPY in his activities because he gets what he gets! God has put a veil over what comes after we die but I'm pretty sure I can guarantee that wearing misery like a cloak in this life, isn't going to help in the next one! As a matter of fact, misery seems to spread like a disease, radiating to all those around. So does happiness! I get to choose which one I'll take up and make mine.

Is it my lot to be happy? Memo to Sue. Be happy. Memo to everyone else. Be happy.

August 14

The Lord roars from Zion

And utters His voice from Jerusalem,

And the heavens and the earth tremble.

But the Lord is a refuge for His people

And a stronghold to the sons of Israel.

Joel 3:16

I was glad to wake up this morning, in the midst of a bad dream. Change is difficult at times and many are the changes taking place these days and I sense it even in my sleep. One thing that doesn't change though, is Jesus Christ. He DOES roar from Zion and the heavens and earth DO tremble. HE is a REFUGE for his people. He is a stronghold, a place of haven that I can go to. He is that place where I can lay down my anxiousness, my sickness, my tiredness, and just simply drink of the water of life. The cost is that I give my life to Him Where better to be than in the refuge that is Jesus Christ? Yours is the same refuge!

August 15

For this reason I also suffer these things, but I am not ashamed; for I know whom I have believed and I am convinced that He is able to guard what I have entrusted to Him until that day.

2 Timothy 1:12

Paul is speaking here of the testimony of the Gospel which he makes declaration of to Timothy. Hmmm. Pondering those words for myself, I DO know whom I have believed and I AM convinced that He is ABLE to guard what I have entrusted to Him. Is He going to do it though? I entrust my family to him. Period. I entrust my work to Him, again no trouble there. I entrust my hopes, my dreams. Wait, what? For me at least, this is a daily, selfish walk of faith....it is the putting in His hands, the very essence of who I am, standing on the belief that He is who He says He is and He will and does, do what He's said He'll do. I guess what I'm trying to say is that I literally daily make the decision to entrust Him with me, the whole package. I'm pretty sure you do the same thing. Now THAT is faith in my book. Pretty sure it's the same in yours.

August 16

"Though He slay me,

I will hope in Him.

Nevertheless I will argue my ways before Him."

This also will be my salvation,

For a godless man may not come before His presence.

Job 13:15-16

I'm hearing a bit about a 'cashless society' lately and have even experienced purchasing from a place that said they would no longer accept 'cash.' Hmmm. I won't tell you what I think about that but I have to say it reminded me of this Scripture. Our money (the paper kind) says 'Legal Tender' on it. That means it may be used to PAY for purchased items. I can choose not to frequent a place if it no longer accepts 'Legal Tender.' If it's a government office I'm pretty sure they can't do that. If it's a privately run establishment, I guess they can say they only accept seashells if they choose.

Job says he has the 'right' to present his case before God. His legal tender is hope and he has the assurance that his particular type of payment is accepted in the Presence of God, in God's store if you will. I have the same tender and so do you.

August 17

Blessed be the Lord, who daily bears our burden,

The God *who* is our salvation. *Selah*

Psalm 68:19

Sometimes I just need to hear that He carries my load every single day. He carries it if I give it to Him.

Most of the time I THINK I can carry my own stuff thank you very much. One must be completely self-sufficient after all says no one ever. That way heads one straight to burn out. Truly so often I loft the particular load I'm finding heaviest to the One who ever shoulders my burden. You know He's always there and He's already carrying my salvation for me. You too!

August 18

For the devious are an abomination to the Lord;

But He is intimate with the upright.

Proverbs 3:32

The literal translation says this:

For the devious are an abomination to the Lord;

But His private counsel is with the upright.

This is where it gets personal. His desire is to speak into those things we hold close, those difficult things that we can't or won't share with anyone. He gets that and in those specific things, He's there to speak life into us. It is THAT counsel that keeps our backs straight and our eyes clear!

August 19

The Lord has bared His holy arm In the sight of all the nations,

That all the ends of the earth may see

The salvation of our God.

Isaiah 52:10

"For I know their works and their thoughts;

The time is coming to gather all nations and tongues.

And they shall come and see My glory.

Isaiah 66:18

You get two Scriptures today.

I cannot imagine what it would look like to "see the salvation of our God" and I must admit, it scares me a bit. One thing I know though is that His ways are always good. I often find myself praying that He would hasten the day of His return. His 'holy arm' in vs. 10 is a metaphor for a warrior who bares His arm for battle. The battle for our salvation has already been won! He SHALL gather all nations and tongues and you know, we shall ALL see His glory!

August 20

Consider it all joy, my brethren, when you encounter various trials, knowing that the testing of your faith produces endurance. And let endurance have *its* perfect result, so that you may be perfect and complete, lacking in nothing.

James 1:2-4

When I receive a bill I wasn't expecting or when the car breaks down or......all of the many things that are annoying....my 'go-to' place often is to swear. Oh, I don't mean swear using God's name because I don't do that. I mean letting those little cracks slip out of my mouth that are not edifying. My mind goes to a place that isn't edifying either. Not always though. There are times when I am able to perceive that it is for endurance's sake that I need to give thanks to God for whatever circumstance I find myself in. It is that endurance that completes my soul and I truly lack in nothing. That's my prayer for each of us today. May endurance have its perfect result so that we may be found perfect and complete, lacking in nothing.

August 21

Fight the good fight of faith; take hold of the eternal life to which you were called, and you made the good confession in the presence of many witnesses.

1 Timothy 6:12

Fighting the 'good fight of faith' shows itself to me in many ways. Sometimes it's forcing me to quit looking at homes for sale on the oceanfront. Sometimes it's praying through a situation for a family member and then praying some more. Sometimes it's choosing to believe that my faith in Jesus Christ is real and has substance and you know sometimes it's just the daily walking out of a choice I made forty-some years ago. Pretty sure it's the same with you.

August 22

Immediately the boy's father cried out and said, "I do believe; help my unbelief."

Mark 9:24

The boy's father, desperately seeking healing for his beloved son, cries in anguish. It is a cry I myself have made more than once. "I do believe; help my unbelief." It is there where God meets me. I needn't believe first nor pretend I believe and then He comes. He comes to my cry. Jesus goes on to say; "All things are possible to him who believes." There exactly is the best place to meet Him.

August 23

For not from the east, nor from the west,

Nor from the desert *comes* exaltation;

But God is the Judge;

He puts down one and exalts another.

But as for me, I will declare *it* forever;

I will sing praises to the God of Jacob.

And all the horns of the wicked He will cut off,

But the horns of the righteous will be lifted up.

Psalm 75:6-7, 9-10

Horns are often used metaphorically in the Scripture to stand for strength and honor. Horns are emblems of power, dominion, glory, and fierceness, as they are the harbinger of attack and defense. The expression "horn of salvation," applied to Christ, is a salvation of strength, or a strong Savior. The Word here is that our 'horns,' those we possess to defend ourselves, demonstrate glory and fierceness, those horns that give us dominion and power and might over those things that seek to harm us... those are OUR horns of righteousness which will be lifted up! We have them from God. As we use them, He WILL lift them up!

August 24

I will extol You, my God, O King,
And I will bless Your name forever and ever.
Every day I will bless You,
And I will praise Your name forever and ever.
Great is the Lord, and highly to be praised,
And His greatness is unsearchable.
One generation shall praise Your works to another, And shall
declare Your mighty acts.
On the glorious splendor of Your majesty
And on Your wonderful works, I will meditate.
Men shall speak of the power of Your awesome acts,
And I will tell of Your greatness.

Psalm 145:1-6

I've been paying special attention to the "one generation shall praise Your works to another" part. In the midst of David's praise to, and blessing of God he makes declaration of his making sure this is generational. It is THIS inheritance that matters! When I am grateful to God, when He has moved on my behalf, when He, when He, and when He.....I want to make sure to shout it to the next generation and the one after that and the one before me (yes, there are still a few of those folks alive!). What an inheritance to speak into someone's life, to make declaration of!

We don't serve a 'one generation' God folks! We serve a God who is the same yesterday, today, and tomorrow. He is for ALL generations and it's been given to us to let people know!

August 25

For if the bugle produces an indistinct sound, who will prepare himself for battle? So also you, unless you utter by the tongue speech that is clear, how will it be known what is spoken? For you will be speaking into the air.

So also you, since you are zealous of spiritual *gifts*, seek to abound for the edification of the church.

1 Corinthians 14:8-9, 12

Have you ever listened to someone and when they were done speaking, had no idea what they'd said? It is frustrating to the listener AND to the speaker. What if, EVERYTHING we spoke was for the edification of the church? What if, we'd been given the power to speak LIFE into people? What if, by our listening, we were able to delve ever deeper into what God has to say to us? We have!

August 26

So rejoice, O sons of Zion,
And be glad in the Lord your God;
For He has given you the early rain for *your* vindication.
And He has poured down for you the rain,
The early and latter rain as before.
"You will have plenty to eat and be satisfied
And praise the name of the Lord your God,
Who has dealt wondrously with you;
Then My people will never be put to shame.
"Thus you will know that I am in the midst of Israel,
And that I am the Lord your God,
And there is no other;
And My people will never be put to shame.

Joel 2:23, 26-27

He makes provision for EVERY season in our lives, both literally and figuratively! Can you imagine a God that both vindicates and makes provision across the ages? What does He require of us for this? Simply that we praise His Name!

The thing that struck me though which He speaks twice of (in other words, PAY ATTENTION) is that we will NEVER be put to shame! Shame is yucky and awful and causes humiliation and guilt and THAT IS NOT the inheritance He has for His people! His provision for us is exonerating, setting us free from the shame of sin and guilt! What a God we serve!

August 27

....."Jacob shall not now be ashamed, nor shall his face now turn pale;

But when he sees his children, the work of My hands, in his midst,

They will sanctify My name;

Indeed, they will sanctify the Holy One of Jacob

And will stand in awe of the God of Israel.

"Those who err in mind will know the truth,

And those who criticize will accept instruction.

Isaiah 29:22-24

The literal translation here is important. "But when he sees his children" literally says; "but when his children see the work of My hands, in his midst."

To see with one's own eyes, the truth of God having fulfilled His Word, to experience it is to make it one's own. Those critical are included in this.

"They will sanctify My name."

AMEN and AMEN!

August 28

Ascribe to the Lord the glory due to His name;

Worship the Lord in holy array.

Psalm 29:2

He has called His people to proclaim His glory;

to worship Him in OUR majesty of holiness! How can this be?

It can be because HE has called us His people to a walk of, and in holiness.

After reading this 'thought' one of my sons responded to me via an email and I couldn't have said it better.

"I like this. I've been thinking a bit recently about how we come into the presence of God. I think we often walk into church without sufficient reverence and trembling fear of the God of the Universe. Chatting or playing on your phone during worship or prayer is ridiculous when you consider how the simple Holy presence of God is enough to strike men dead!"

August 29

It shall come about, when I bring a cloud over the earth, that the bow will be seen in the cloud, and I will remember My covenant, which is between Me and you and every living creature of all flesh; and never again shall the water become a flood to destroy all flesh. When the bow is in the cloud, then I will look upon it, to remember the everlasting covenant between God and every living creature of all flesh that is on the earth."

Genesis 9:14-16

It doesn't say here that the rainbow is for us. God says He's reminding Himself of the everlasting covenant He's made with all flesh on the earth to never flood the earth again. In the very reminding of God, He blesses us with beauty. If He sets something in the sky to remind Himself, do you think He doesn't appreciate our reminding Him of His promises? May it never be! For me, and I believe for you too, a good way to begin a prayer to God is to say: "It says in your Word...." He stands on it and so do we!

August 30

He has made known to His people the power of His works,
In giving them the heritage of the nations.

Psalm 111:6

Lately, I've been focusing it seems on heritage or inheritance.
The word actually is defined as:

Something that is handed down from the past, as a tradition:

Something that comes or belongs to one by reason of birth;
an inherited lot or portion

Something reserved for one

Something that has been or may be inherited by legal
descent or succession.

Sue's translation:

He has shown us and told us the power of His works by giving
us the right, by reason of birth in Him, to have the heirship
of the nations!

Our ancestry leads straight back to Him and includes each
of us folks! Can you imagine? A family of God. Well actually,
THE family of God!

August 31

He has made His wonders to be remembered;

The Lord is gracious and compassionate.

Psalm 111:4

I ask myself, do I remember His wonders? In the midst of my constant 'asking' for what seems to be important, what I deem to be critical each day; do I remember His wonders. Sad to say I do not but you know I will get better at it. He IS gracious and He IS compassionate. To think on His wonders escorts me into the Holy of Holies and it is a pleasant place to be folks, it is a pleasant place to be.

September

September 01

When Jesus saw him lying *there*, and knew that he had already been a long time *in that condition*, He said to him, "Do you wish to get well?" The sick man answered Him, "Sir, I have no man to put me into the pool when the water is stirred up, but while I am coming, another steps down before me." Jesus said to him, "Get up, pick up your pallet and walk." Immediately the man became well, and picked up his pallet and *began* to walk.

John 5:6-9

I'm not writing about the man's healing. I'm writing about the response Jesus made to the man. It is Him we are to be like and it is His Holy Spirit in us that is our enablement. Often when I pray for someone, it is: Please Jesus, heal...." or "Jesus, please continue with this healing" and that is what is required. Other times though, it is to SPEAK the words: "Get up, pick up your pallet and walk." This is in no way meant to lay a trip on anyone and how they are to pray. This is also not the politically correct nor popular way to pray these days. Speaking in the authority of God into someone's life is risky and perhaps sets one up for embarrassment. It also speaks life into those who need to hear, because the hearing of the words is the power to set someone on their feet. Jesus did it and by the Power of His Holy Spirit, the Helper, so must we.

September 02

Now to Him who is able to keep you from stumbling, and to make you stand in the presence of His glory blameless with great joy, to the only God our Savior, through Jesus Christ our Lord, *be* glory, majesty, dominion and authority, before all time and now and forever. Amen.

Jude 24-25

It is difficult for me to comprehend this. The magnitude of it is more than I've ever hoped for. This is for eternity folks and it's yours too. I can only imagine.

Now to Him be glory, majesty, dominion, and authority before all time, now and to all the ages. He keeps me from stumbling and makes me stand in the presence of His glory, blameless, with great joy. You too! AMEN!

September 03

"Pay attention to Me, O My people,

And give ear to Me, O My nation;

For a law will go forth from Me,

And I will set My justice for a light of the peoples.

For I am the Lord your God, who stirs up the sea and its waves roar (the Lord of hosts is His name). I have put My words in your mouth and have covered you with the shadow of My hand, to establish the heavens, to found the earth, and to say to Zion, 'You are My people.'"

Isaiah 51:4, 15-16

Sue's translation:

Pay attention you who call on My Name!

Listen to Me my people!

I give you My Law,

Setting justice as the light to lead you.

I am YOUR God who empowers the sea, my Name is GOD! I HAVE PUT MY WORDS IN YOUR MOUTH AND HAVE COVERED YOU with the covering of My hand to establish the heavens, found the earth, and to say to you, "YOU ARE MY PEOPLE!"

JUSTICE has been given to us!

September 04

You shall love the Lord your God with all your heart and with all your soul and with all your might. These words, which I am commanding you today, shall be on your heart. You shall teach them diligently to your sons and shall talk of them when you sit in your house and when you walk by the way and when you lie down and when you rise up.

Deuteronomy 6:5-7

This is where it gets real. This is living the dream and the dream is Jesus Christ. I love my sons fiercely. I desire the very best for them and if there has been a reason to live this Scripture and make it my own, it's so that they too understand its value and live by it, make it a part of them. The bonus is, it has become a part of me too.

September 05

As for me, I shall behold Your face in righteousness;

I will be satisfied with Your likeness when I awake.

Psalm 17:15

David is speaking here of his inheritance in God. He says upon waking (when we are ready to put on our work shoes and capture the world....) he will be SATISFIED with beholding Your likeness!

He makes a declaration that God is where he is satiated, not by what his accomplishments of the day may bring.

There is a walking in the Presence of God here which He has made available for each of us!

Such a simple thing to be satisfied with, yet so often He eludes me, or rather I should say, I try to elude Him. This Scripture is a decision I must continually make. I will be SATISFIED with His likeness! Methinks, you too!

September 06

Train up a child in the way he should go,

Even when he is old he will not depart from it.

Proverbs 22:6

This translation isn't exact. It literally says:

Train up a child according to his way,

Even when he is old he will not depart from it.

Another version translates it as:

Train up the child according to the tenor of his way, and when he is old he will not depart from it.

Does this mean we should teach children to do what they want? May it never be!

Just as God leads us when we listen, to use those very natural gifts which He's given us to glorify and praise Him so we too, need to encourage children in the very things, those excellent, specific gifts which God has given each of them as a way to glorify God, each in his or her own uniqueness! What one loves, what one is able to use for the glory of God, ah, one will never depart from it!

September 07

Where can we go up? Our brethren have made our hearts melt, saying, "The people are bigger and taller than we; the cities are large and fortified to heaven. And besides, we saw the sons of the Anakim there."' Then I said to you, 'Do not be shocked, nor fear them. The Lord your God who goes before you will Himself fight on your behalf, just as He did for you in Egypt before your eyes, and in the wilderness where you saw how the Lord your God carried you, just as a man carries his son, in all the way which you have walked until you came to this place.' But for all this, you did not trust the Lord your God, who goes before you on *your* way, to seek out a place for you to encamp, in fire by night and cloud by day, to show you the way in which you should go.

Deuteronomy 1:28-33

Why this? This because it is what so many say, including me....

"The people are bigger than me; the work is too hard. And besides, I saw someone I don't want to associate with there. Yes I know you helped me in the past,....but I'm just not sure and I'm afraid, or I'm too tired or I don't believe."

Either the promises of God are true or they aren't. It simply can't be that just some of them are true...the ones that are easiest to follow. Either He goes before us to seek out a place for us or He doesn't. He shows the way we should go. Period. It's our responsibility to simply go.

September 08

To the pure, all things are pure; but to those who are defiled and unbelieving, nothing is pure, but both their mind and their conscience are defiled.

Titus 1:15

I have never used this 'thought.' That surprises me. This speaks about the state one is in.

I'm reminded of an experience I had as a 12 year old. I was on a bus and everyone had gotten off but me and it was dark outside. The driver was the owner of the local roller-skating rink which I had attended and I was to be the last one off. He asked me if I'd like to come up and sit on his lap while he drove "because all girls like to sit on men's laps." I was thoroughly disgusted and afraid as you can imagine. My response was a weak "No thanks." but I never forgot it and for many years, because of it, I distrusted pretty much any man older than me.

It is possible to go from a defiled state to a pure state. The way to do that is through the Blood of the Lamb. He turns shame and hate, bitterness and sorrow into that which is whole and healed and pure. That's the God we serve and I'm so grateful I know Him. I'm glad you do to.

261

September 09

The generous man will be prosperous,

And he who waters will himself be watered.

Proverbs 11:25

Literal translation:

The soul of blessing will be made fat,

And he who waters will himself be watered.

It doesn't say here folks that the one who waters will receive from the one he watered. That's God's business. We're to pour out, knowing that it will be showered back on us by whomever or whatever He chooses.

The bottom line is to be generous, to give with all one's might. The result is to be watered from a well that never runs dry.

September 10

Then Jesus was led up by the Spirit into the wilderness to be tempted by the devil. And after He had fasted forty days and forty nights, He then became hungry. And the tempter came and said to Him, "If You are the Son of God, command that these stones become bread." But He answered and said, "It is written, 'Man shall not live on bread alone, but on every word that proceeds out of the mouth of God.'"

Matthew 4:1-4

I very seldom wake up with a 'thought.' This is an exception. On the surface, this is pretty cut and dried. We require the Word of God for our very existence. Yes! Of course we do! The Word tells us that by faith, we can command mountains to move! It seems to me, herein lies the meat of this. SHOULD WE, as sons and daughters of God, be commanding mountains to move or stones to become bread to serve ourselves or to serve God? If it's the latter, AMEN and AMEN! If it's the former, we need to recognize the commanding for what it is....simply a way to fill our bellies. God wants more than that for His people. He wants us to walk in the power of EVERY WORD THAT PROCEEDS OUT OF HIS MOUTH, commanding by faith, according to what the Scripture says, not what we say! That is exactly what Jesus did.

September 11

And inasmuch as it is appointed for men to die once and after this *comes* judgment, so Christ also, having been offered once to bear the sins of many, will appear a second time for salvation without *reference to* sin, to those who eagerly await Him.

Hebrews 9:27-28

Wait. WHAT? Does this say that I'm to be judged WHEN I die? I don't get to 'get better' once I've been taken to heaven? I believe it does. In the here and now, how comfortable am I with God? Do I 'like' to spend time with Him because if I don't, it won't bode well for me to spend eternity with Him.

I've heard couples and/or friends recount the many years they've spent with their loved ones and how over those years, they've come to know better and love more deeply. You know I get that. Make no mistake. He WILL APPEAR to bring salvation to those who wait for Him. I want to know Him before He gets here. Pretty sure you do too.

September 12

Salvation belongs to the Lord;

Your blessing *be* upon Your people! *Selah.*

Psalm 3:8

Literal translation:

Deliverance belongs to the Lord;

Your blessing is upon Your people! Selah.

I equate salvation with the past. I am saved for what's ahead and yes of course; that is true. Here though, the word "deliverance" speaks of setting free, liberating from what 'continues' to hold me down. I am not only saved, I am DELIVERED!

I look to people and/or money, sometimes...time, to deliver me from circumstances which aren't to my liking; things I wish to escape from for one reason or another. True deliverance though, comes from just one place and by faith, I need to accept that it is in HIS perfect timing, not mine. I get to be refined and how He chooses to do it is His business. His promise is that His blessing 'is' (present tense) upon me and that deliverance comes from His hand alone. Accepting that is walking by faith, not in what I see but by what I know. Pretty sure it's the same for you.

September 13

That which is born of the flesh is flesh, and that which is born
of the Spirit is spirit. Do not be amazed that I said to you,
'You must be born again.' The wind blows where it wishes
and you hear the sound of it, but do not know where it comes
from and where it is going; so is everyone who is born of the
Spirit."

John 3:6-8

The literal translation of vs. 7 is "You must be born from
above." Here once again is a faith and trust issue. Spirit like
the wind, blows where it wishes, taking us with it and in it.
Just like the wind, we who are born of His Spirit, experience
it but it is not given to us to know where it is taking us. It's
called faith. Our walk in Jesus Christ is not by sight but by
faith that He will blow us where we need to go for His
purposes, not ours.

September 14

Have I not commanded you? Be strong and courageous! Do not tremble or be dismayed, for the Lord your God is with you wherever you go."

Joshua 1:9

Today you get two 'thoughts'. This is about the faithfulness of God. The first relates God's Word to Joshua upon the death of Moses, to give the people possession of the land promised them.

That same promise, that same inheritance has been fulfilled for us in Jesus Christ.

In Him, you also, after listening to the message of truth, the gospel of your salvation—having also believed, you were sealed in Him with the Holy Spirit of promise, who is given as a pledge of our inheritance, with a view to the redemption of *God's own* possession, to the praise of His glory.

Ephesians 1:13-14

We no longer are required to 'go' to a land. We ARE the land! AMEN!

September 15

When a strong *man*, fully armed, guards his own house, his possessions are undisturbed. But when someone stronger than he attacks him and overpowers him, he takes away from him all his armor on which he had relied and distributes his plunder. He who is not with Me is against Me; and he who does not gather with Me, scatters.

Luke 11:21-23

If there is a Scripture that needs to be conveyed to generations to come, it is this one. Guard your house people! Teach your children to post a guard over their loved ones! PRAY PROTECTION, PRAY FAITH, PRAY HOPE, AND PRAY FOR GOD'S PRESENCE!

God CANNOT be overcome! Whoever isn't for Him, is against Him!

September 16

For I have come to have much joy and comfort in your love, because the hearts of the saints have been refreshed through you, brother.

Philemon 1:7

Paul is expressing the joy and comfort he's received from Philemon and tells him that the saints also have been refreshed through him. Have you ever been around those ones who by the very act of being with them, you come alive? You smile when you think of them and truly, they invigorate, rejuvenate your very soul? Oh, what a true saint of God Philemon must have been! I pray that each of us may have that same spirit to bring refreshment, joy, and comfort to those around us! To give life to others through the Holy Spirit!

September 17

But Ruth said, "Do not urge me to leave you *or* turn back from following you; for where you go, I will go, and where you lodge, I will lodge. Your people *shall be* my people, and your God, my God.

Ruth 1:16

I have never used this verse nor for that matter, this book of the Bible before. Why now? Well, I've been giving a bit of thought to those one holds dear. Brothers, sisters, sisters and brothers-in-law, in-laws, outlaws....you get the picture. One cherishes them, stays close if not in location, certainly in one's heart. There are those too, whom God puts in our path for a purpose. Oftentimes we come to cherish them, hold them dear, because they define for us, who we are, and in some cases, what we have or will become.

So often I've heard this Scripture in the form of a song (sung at the wedding of yours truly many years ago by two dear brothers from Christian Family Farm). This isn't the reference in the Bible though. As you know, it was used by a daughter-in-law who directed it toward her dead husband's mother. No blood relation, none. God put them together for a specific purpose and in this case, it was ultimately to produce a lineage that included both David and Jesus. God always has a plan for joining us with those dear to us. What He does for us is always good, always fruitful.

Whether by blood, by Spirit, or both, I'm grateful for those God has joined me to. The Body of Christ. I'm ever so thankful.

September 18

How blessed will you be, you who sow beside all waters,

Who let out freely the ox and the donkey.

Isaiah 32:20

It is easy to water a garden with nice, straight rows, especially when one is told where best to water. It becomes successively more difficult as the plantings are cast here and there with no rhyme or reason. Same with tilling the soil. One wouldn't typically plant in a scattered fashion. We aren't called to sow only where the rows are straight. We are called to sow beside ALL waters. We are called to let out our proverbial ox and our donkey FREELY! We GET TO sow by dirty waters too that have made us sick and have hurt us because the power of God can make those waters clean! Here again, is a walk in faith. It is believing that by the Spirit of Jesus Christ, God will cause our sowing to bear fruit.

September 19

Anxiety in a man's heart weighs it down,

But a good word makes it glad.

Proverbs 12:25

I wasn't looking for this 'thought' this morning and yet it found me! Anxiety is defined as distress or uneasiness caused by fear of danger or misfortune. To put it another way, anxiety is simply the casting aside of faith that God is sufficient in His care of us.

The 'glad' news is that He IS who He says He is and He will do what He says He'll do. He has our back, always!

September 20

Now Nadab and Abihu, the sons of Aaron, took their respective firepans, and after putting fire in them, placed incense on it and offered strange fire before the Lord, which He had not commanded them. And fire came out from the presence of the Lord and consumed them, and they died before the Lord. Then Moses said to Aaron, "It is what the Lord spoke, saying,

'By those who come near Me I will be treated as holy,

And before all the people I will be honored.'"

So Aaron, therefore, kept silent.

Leviticus 10:1-3

It seems to me that we don't get to do whatever we want to do, however we want to do it. The King's business has to be done the King's way. We bring too much of our opinion into the House of God and we sit back in a corner talking about how "I think things ought to be done." That is 'strange fire.' God doesn't care what we think. This isn't about what we like. It's about what God chooses to use to accomplish His will and much of our own opinion is 'strange fire.' It's killing our preachers, our churches and it's killing us, our effectiveness. When we allow the world to dictate to us, we might please the world but we lose the Presence of God because His is a Holy Place.

September 21

Do not be hasty in word or impulsive in thought to bring up a matter in the presence of God. For God is in heaven and you are on the earth; therefore let your words be few. For the dream comes through much effort and the voice of a fool through many words.

Ecclesiastes 5:2-3

I get the 'do not be hasty with your mouth' part when I speak with God. The 'hurry your heart to bring up a matter' part though, is more difficult for me. God cares about the trivial stuff. It's rather that He desires to give me what I've asked for so I need to be very sure before I ask. It is a serious thing to put something before the throne of grace! Let my heart be sure, and my words be few, and let my prayers be effectual rather than simply numerous. Yours too.

September 22

The way of a guilty man is crooked,

But as for the pure, his conduct is upright.

Proverbs 21:8

Last evening I wanted to share with my dear husband what I thought was a profound truth pertaining to social justice. At the time he was watching something on his laptop and said, "I'm watching something. Maybe later."

The retort that immediately popped into my head was:

"When I die, you'll be sorry you didn't listen to me more often because then it'll be too late."

G.U.I.L.T.

I laugh when I think about it. So often my (perhaps 'our') motivation or response is to 'guilt' someone into something. Had I made that remark, I surely would have gotten a response from him but I'm pretty sure it wouldn't have been what I was looking for, which was affirmation. God gets what guilt is because He's made a way to rid us of its evil snare. When guilt is used to push one into something, to manipulate...the fruit of it is never good. You know I never did get around to telling him about my 'profound' thought but I'm pretty sure if it's important enough, I will.

September 23

Let no one deceive you with empty words, for because of these things the wrath of God comes upon the sons of disobedience.

Ephesians 5:6

One of my sons uses the expression: "I know right well..." What a great expression! YES! Each of us does know 'right well' with an emphasis on the 'right.' Some things are easy to peg. Some other things not so much. Empty means literally: 'containing nothing.' We are not to listen to, nor be deceived by words which contain nothing, no value, no content, no faith, no hope, no life. Good words to live by.

September 24

If the axe is dull and he does not sharpen *its* edge, then he must exert more strength. Wisdom has the advantage of giving success.

Ecclesiastes 10:10

I love this Scripture! I try to live in a black and white world....not a grey one. It applies to just about everything I do and say. If I am dull and a slacker; if I am not speaking life, not only does it take more strength to maintain the load, chop the 'wood' (or carry on the conversation), it also gets me off the path that I need to be on, focusing on what is good and true and right....on the path that leads me to Him! Let's sharpen our axes, shall we?

September 25

Therefore if you have been raised up with Christ, keep seeking the things above, where Christ is, seated at the right hand of God. Set your mind on the things above, not on the things that are on earth. For you have died and your life is hidden with Christ in God.

Colossians 3:1-3

It is relatively easy to seek what is in front of you.....after all, there it is and it doesn't take THAT much effort. We are called though, to keep seeking that place where Christ is, to experience a life hidden with Him in God. For me, this means to not let the cares of the day nor the worries of the night, nor the distractions for that matter, take ahold of me....but rather to continually seek where and what HIS place is for me! Here's an illustration.

I was grumbling to myself while I was cleaning the toilet and bathroom. Right before attending to it, I'd read the Scripture about "He who is not with Me is against Me," from Luke:11. It dawned on me that instead of grumbling, being squarely focused on myself, I should be praying for the person someone had asked me to pray for and specifically on this day. Problem solved on all accounts. It's pretty difficult to keep one's eyes on oneself whilst praying unless of course one grumbles to God and trust me, He can take it much better than I can and He knows what to do with it.

September 26

"But as for me, I would seek God,

And I would place my cause before God;

Who does great and unsearchable things,

Wonders without number.

"So the helpless has hope,

And unrighteousness must shut its mouth.

Job 5:8-9, 16

God puts me in a tight box sometimes. I'm pretty good at trying to figure out my own way...my own problems...at least I think I am. Sometimes the only way I'll pay attention is for Him to give me absolutely no other alternative than to turn to Him. It's a good, painful place to be in, solely dependent upon His leading, His mercy, His grace. His ways are truly unfathomable and the result which He brings me to every single time is hope in Him. Unrighteousness must indeed, shut its mouth.

Hope reigns supreme!

September 27

The merciful man does himself good,

But the cruel man does himself harm.

Proverbs 11:17

Mercy is defined as showing compassionate or kindly forbearance toward an offender.

Cruelty comes in many forms. Emotional blackmail, withholding favor, and hard-heartedness are a few which come to mind. Each is a way that causes suffering. Anger poured out like a hot flame is another. Showing mercy though is like a salve that quenches a burning itch or like a pleasant aroma that makes one simply want to stand and draw it in. Mercy is a healer of the soul and it is what every person must have to be whole.

Showing mercy isn't conditional for those being shown it. There are no criteria that one has to meet to be shown mercy and it tops getting even, every single time.

September 28

Then the Lord spoke to Moses, saying, "Speak to Aaron and to his sons, saying, 'Thus you shall bless the sons of Israel. You shall say to them:

The Lord bless you, and keep you;

The Lord make His face shine on you,

And be gracious to you;

The Lord lift up His countenance on you,

And give you peace.'

So they shall invoke My name on the sons of Israel, and I *then* will bless them."

Numbers 6:22-27

These are OUR words folks! This is God's intent for His people! May they bless you and keep you and your house.

AMEN!

September 29

The way of a fool is right in his own eyes,

But a wise man is he who listens to counsel.

Proverbs 12:15

Have you ever laid in bed at night rehashing a discussion you've had during the day, mentally building your case against him or her, arguing in your mind as to why you are correct and that person is wrong? Well, I have and it leaves me exhausted. My dear husband has done it too and as a matter of principle, we try not to discuss these kinds of issues before going to bed because we KNOW the result will be little or no sleep! There is almost nothing worse than self-righteousness. It reeks of selfishness and is not good for the soul. It's even worse when one is aware that someone else is doing exactly this because if it is pointed out to that person, the one who does the pointing out becomes the object of anger while adding yet more self-righteous fuel to the fire already well burning!

September 30

"Hear, O kings; give ear, O rulers!

I—to the Lord, I will sing,

I will sing praise to the Lord, the God of Israel.

"Thus let all Your enemies perish, O Lord;

But let those who love Him be like the rising of the sun in its might."

And the land was undisturbed for forty years.

Judges 5:3, 31

I seem to say quite a few 'I's' these days. 'I' this and 'I' that. I hear a few 'you's' too but they aren't often directed toward the Lord. I love this Scripture! It is a cry to battle! A cry before God! Let my 'I' be rather to Him. Let my song be directed toward Him and let it be a battle cry!

".....and the land was undisturbed for forty years."

October

October 01

Like a city that is broken into *and* without walls

Is a man who has no control over his spirit.

Proverbs 25:28

My thoughts are usually filled with 'not we but He.' In this instance though, the expectation is 'we' and then 'He.' It is an instruction to us.... simply a warning. When there is no control, no restraint nor discipline in a man, he becomes vulnerable. It is a sobering place to be and a place where there is murkiness and no clarity to stand on the Word of God. It is a good word to take to heart.

Every day my life is full of decisions. God has given me the power to decide how strong the walls of my spirit are. I get to choose and so do you.

October 02

For you were called to freedom, brethren; only *do* not *turn* your freedom into an opportunity for the flesh, but through love serve one another. For the whole Law is fulfilled in one word, in the *statement*, "You shall love your neighbor as yourself." But if you bite and devour one another, take care that you are not consumed by one another.

Galatians 5:13-15

I have no problem loving my family, even when I'm 'annoyed' with them. I don't have a problem loving friends nor even folks I don't know. It's those people that are jerks that I have a problem with! I find myself wanting to take on the "What did I ever do to you?" attitude. It's those people who put themselves first, that gets me going!

Well, when I let MY attitude get in the way of loving someone as I love myself, I'm doing exactly what I abhor by putting ME before THEM. I am turning the grace that God gave me to love, into an opportunity for my flesh to go into 'hurt' mode or even into 'bitterness' mode. Do I allow myself to be consumed by anger, pain, and anguish toward another, or rather do I chose to love as I love myself; to serve as I serve myself? Here then is the freedom of Jesus Christ, to love my neighbor (friend, family, the guy next door or, someone who belittles me, has caused me heartache and pain) as myself.

October 03

"For the mountains may be removed and the hills may shake,

But My lovingkindness will not be removed from you,

And My covenant of peace will not be shaken,"

Says the Lord who has compassion on you.

Isaiah 54:10

Who believes this? I don't often think of God's 'covenant of peace' with me. Okay, never. I get the 'lovingkindness' part and I take it, and make it mine....but peace? Really?

The dictionary defines peace as:

Cessation of or freedom from any strife or dissension.

Freedom of the mind from annoyance, distraction, anxiety, an obsession, etc.; tranquility; serenity.

HE says HIS lovingkindness AND His covenant of peace will NOT BE SHAKEN. When I seem to throw it back in His face because of unbelief, He shows me compassion. This is my truth and it's yours too.

October 04

You have tried my heart;

You have visited *me* by night;

You have tested me and You find nothing;

I have purposed that my mouth will not transgress.

Keep me as the apple of the eye;

Hide me in the shadow of Your wings

Psalm 17:3,8

I hope that in eternity I will get the chance to meet David. He has ever been my hero because of his unabashed love for God. So often I can identify with his words.

"You have tried my heart;

You have visited me by night;"

I'm not sure about the "You have tested me and You found nothing;" or the "I have purposed that my mouth that I will not transgress." part but God knows my heart for sure.

"Keep me as the apple of the eye;

Hide me in the shadow of Your wings."

I almost feel like I need permission to pray these things and yet, there is David and you know, if he can, so can I. Pretty sure you can too.

October 05

Will they not go astray who devise evil?

But kindness and truth *will be to* those who devise good.

Proverbs 14:22

I haven't used this 'thought' before. How can that be? I am well able to 'devise' good for those I like/love. I'm even able to do it for those that are strangers. SOMETIMES I can do it for folks that I prefer not to be around. Oh, I can justify myself by saying I'm not actively devising evil toward those ones.....hmmmm. Here though is another way. I am called to plan, contrive, 'devise' good. Period. I'm pretty sure that means the guy that just pulled in front of me, the person who told an untruth about me, that one who maligned me where I had no guilt. It means that one that hurts me, whenever I think of them, and not the kind of pain that is a good, clean pain which results in healing but rather the kind of pain that makes me feel small and unloved; it is those folks that as I walk in faith, Jesus Christ pushes; no demands me to devise good for. What do I get in return? The God of the universe gives me kindness and truth! Can you imagine! What a deal! It's your deal too!

October 06

"But I say to you who hear, love your enemies, do good to those who hate you, bless those who curse you, pray for those who mistreat you. Whoever hits you on the cheek, offer him the other also; and whoever takes away your coat, do not withhold your shirt from him either. Give to everyone who asks of you, and whoever takes away what is yours, do not demand it back. Treat others the same way you want them to treat you. If you love those who love you, what credit is *that* to you? For even sinners love those who love them.

Luke 6:27-32

I know that you've heard me say this before but it bears repeating. Don't give with the expectation to receive back from the person you gave to, or from anyone else for that matter. God is the giver and when you take it into your own hands, what you receive back is done on earth, not in heaven. Trust me when I say this: God's return is much greater than anything you can receive here. I speak to you and to me both. It is a valuable lesson to learn and one which each of us needs to be reminded of.

October 07

Then the sons of Joseph spoke to Joshua, saying, "Why have you given me only one lot and one portion for an inheritance, since I am a numerous people whom the Lord has thus far blessed?" Joshua said to them, "If you are a numerous people, go up to the forest and clear a place for yourself there in the land of the Perizzites and of the Rephaim, since the hill country of Ephraim is too narrow for you." The sons of Joseph said, "The hill country is not enough for us, and all the Canaanites who live in the valley land have chariots of iron, both those who are in Beth-shean and its towns and those who are in the valley of Jezreel." Joshua spoke to the house of Joseph, to Ephraim and Manasseh, saying, "You are a numerous people and have great power; you shall not have one lot *only*, but the hill country shall be yours. For though it is a forest, you shall clear it, and to its farthest borders it shall be yours; for you shall drive out the Canaanites, even though they have chariots of iron *and* though they are strong."

Joshua 17:14-18

SOMETIMES, there is a cost to an inheritance. SOMETIMES it seems not worth the effort. SOMETIMES to gain what it is, I must climb steep proverbial hills, cut down trees, clear the land, suffer illness, feel the despair of a job seemingly never to be finished......with my goal never to be reached.

Ah, but when I press toward the mark....reach the goal, the result is that I come to that place where the air is clear and the breeze is fresh. Where my perspective is much wider and more grand than I ever could have imagined. Where the rain touches my face directly from the Hand of God....and THAT my friends, is my inheritance from God. It's yours too!

October 08

Here is what I have seen to be good and fitting: to eat, to drink and enjoy oneself in all one's labor in which he toils under the sun *during* the few years of his life which God has given him; for this is his reward.

Ecclesiastes 5:18

I've never particularly cared for this Scripture because I've thought Solomon must have been in a particularly bad mood when he wrote it. Rather fatalistic it seemed. Perhaps I haven't understood what he was saying.

The literal translation says:

"Here is what I have seen to be good and beautiful: to eat, to drink and see good....."

The "see good" part is what is the crux of this Word. This isn't saying that I should have an overgrown sense of pride in what I've done....no! It's speaking of having the sense to recognize that what I've done, has been good BECAUSE God has given it to me to do! Even when at times, I've hated the work, despised the tediousness of it, denied the praise from others because of it, and when it has seemed that the fruit of it has been folly! The thing is.....since I've gotten to know Him, it's ALWAYS been HIS WORK! It is the knowing that my 'share' has been from Him and for Him HIS WORK was, is, and will be....good and beautiful. What a reward! You get it too!

October 09

For in many dreams and in many words there is emptiness. Rather, fear God.

Ecclesiastes 5:7

Let me say, "AMEN." Speak less, pray more.

October 10

I love the Lord, because He hears

My voice *and* my supplications.

Because He has inclined His ear to me,

Therefore I shall call *upon Him* as long as I live.

Psalm 116:1-2

Sometimes I need to say things that either I'm too embarrassed to share with others or I think they simply wouldn't want to listen to. When I accepted Jesus Christ into my heart and my life that changed. Since then I've had a constant companion.....One who I can share my joys, my sorrows, my hopes and dreams with. One who never makes fun of our conversation and, One who really listens to me. David has the boldness to say, "Because He has inclined His ear to me, ...I shall call upon Him as long as I live." What an excellent word! He does incline His ear to me. You too!

October 11

He has told you, O man, what is good;

And what does the Lord require of you

But to do justice, to love kindness,

And to walk humbly with your God?

Micah 6:8

I woke up with this 'thought' on my heart. God was 'annoyed' with His people Israel when these words were spoken. This is what He questioned them with....what they needed to do.

Do justice. Love kindness. Walk humbly with your God. This isn't rocket science folks. As I've said before, I live in a pretty black and white world and these words are life to me. They are just clean and straight! Do what is just and right. Love kindness....be loyal to those God has given you; your family and those in the family of God which He's given you. Walk humbly with your God....in a prudent, well-considered way. That's it.

October 12

Whoever forces you to go one mile, go with him two.

Matthew 5:41

I hate being forced to do anything. One might say I have 'control' issues.

I married very young and consequently divorced also very young. A few years later I accepted Jesus Christ as my savior, having been led to Him kicking and screaming! Flash forward. My ex-husband married which freed me in my way of thinking, to do the same. I became acquainted with another 'fella' and the rest is history. The part about getting married again was difficult, to say the least.

The morning of my wedding I was having none of it. While the Holy Spirit was pushing me to do it, I was pushing right back. You see 'once burned, twice learned' had been my motto and I was convinced that I was making a really dumb mistake yet again.

There is another way though.....it's the way of bringing the Holy Spirit into the equation. It's the giving of control to the One who gave me my life back. It's the walking by faith, believing that Jesus Christ is who He says He is and will take me where I need to go with whomever He chooses me to be with. Period. That was forty-some years ago and yep, it's true.

October 13

This I recall to my mind,

Therefore I have hope.

The Lord's lovingkindnesses indeed never cease,

For His compassions never fail.

They are new every morning;

Great is Your faithfulness.

"The Lord is my portion," says my soul,

"Therefore I have hope in Him."

Lamentations 3:21-24

When I'm in a bad mood I get pretty quiet, to the point that one of my sons says I 'stomp around and don't talk.' I'll admit it. In my defense, it's my coping mechanism which (darn it) that son doesn't let me get away with. When I'm in that state, it is hard to switch gears; that getting in a 'good mood' whilst still in a 'bad mood.'

This is one of those 'help' places I go to do it. This Scripture stops self-pity in its tracks. It builds up my faith and fills me with the reality that yes, He IS my Portion! I DO have hope in Him! His lovingkindness NEVER stops, his compassion never fails! I get a new start every morning! So do you!

October 14

"As for you, son of man, describe the temple to the house of Israel, that they may be ashamed of their iniquities; and let them measure the plan. If they are ashamed of all that they have done, make known to them the design of the house, its structure, its exits, its entrances, all its designs, all its statutes, and all its laws. And write *it* in their sight, so that they may observe its whole design and all its statutes and do them. This is the law of the house: its entire area on the top of the mountain all around *shall be* most holy. Behold, this is the law of the house.

Ezekiel 43:10-12

Why this thought, this description of God's 'house'? He wanted to show them where He lived, the perfection built to His exact specifications. His 'place.'

When one really knows a house, they know each room, each little nook, each cranny....one discovers why the house is special and ultimately one grows to love the house. One is familiar with it and tends it, cares for it, and makes it the place where there is peace. It is a place where one finds protection and rest and solace for one's soul. Each of us has the choice to live in God's house. Yes it is true it is no longer a temple on a mountain. Now its Name is Jesus Christ and let me tell you, it is a pleasant place to live

October 15

For He rescued us from the domain of darkness, and transferred us to the kingdom of His beloved Son, in whom we have redemption, the forgiveness of sins.

Colossians 1:13-14

Our family moved many times when I was young and I truly hated it. It always scared me and was painful. Since then, it's mostly been a hassle, whether it's a new place or whether it's a new situation. I've moved because I wanted to and sometimes because I've had to.

One weeds through all of one's stuff, hoping to get rid of the 'stuff' collected and not made use of, or because the 'stuff' has become a weight around the neck.

I've often brought 'stuff' along that needs to be thrown away, both mentally and physically.

Sometimes I've needed to move on in my spirit, so that God can take me to another place, perhaps where I wouldn't have chosen to go. The thing is, wherever I end up, He's put me there. It's in the light where He lives, where I am secure and more importantly, where I have redemption, and where I am forgiven.....It's a safe place and it is ever, a good move!

October 16

All Scripture is inspired by God and profitable for teaching, for reproof, for correction, for training in righteousness; so that the man of God may be adequate, equipped for every good work.

2 Timothy 3:16-17

I don't always believe that I am adequate nor that I am equipped for every good work.

This Scripture exactly describes why it is important for each of us to read the Word for ourselves, to not get it second-hand.

It can be explained to a person how to drive a car including the rules associated with it but if they don't drive themselves, they won't be able to do it.

The Scriptures make me adequate. They equip me for every good work. They've taught me how to 'drive.' You too.

October 17

For by one offering He has perfected for all time those who are sanctified.

And the Holy Spirit also testifies to us; for after saying,

. "This is the covenant that I will make with them

After those days, says the Lord:

I will put My laws upon their heart,

And on their mind I will write them,"

He then says,

"And their sins and their lawless deeds

I will remember no more."

Now where there is forgiveness of these things, there is no longer *any* offering for sin.

Hebrews 10:14-18

Earlier in this chapter regarding blood sacrifice, it says; "But in those *sacrifices* there is a reminder of sins year by year." This is exactly what Jesus came to do away with! When He forgives our sins, He does not throw them repeatedly, in our face! No keeping track! Let me suggest here that even as He doesn't keep track of our sins, neither should we keep track of the sins of others nor remind them. No reminders!

October 18

He will cover you with His pinions,

And under His wings you may seek refuge;

His faithfulness is a shield and bulwark.

Psalm 91:4

This is such a simple Word. Sometimes I just need a place where I'm safe....not judged, not scolded, a place where I don't have to be strong. To be honest, I don't always feel like I have that place when I'm being bombarded with the cares of the world to the point that I just want to sleep or hide in a hole to make it stop. That's when I truly need that refuge, that place where the cares of the world just can't reach me, where I can let down my guard. I have a place like that. It IS where there is a shield over me and a wall around me and I am secure with One who always seeks my good. I just need to go there. When I do, it is always good and there is a view too! You have that place, I know it.

October 19

Wrath is fierce and anger is a flood,

But who can stand before jealousy?

Proverbs 27:4

I am not jealous of those with more wealth nor fame nor power than me. Maybe it's because God took me out of the mire and muck and brought me to that place where I am clean.

It isn't that I haven't felt jealousy mind you. It seeps in like a fog and before I know it, I'm 'wishing' for what God hasn't given me freely. Therein lies the trouble. Jealousy says that my Provider hasn't given me my just reward, He hasn't given me what is fair. It causes hurt and anger. Jesus Christ didn't come to bring fairness, and by fairness, I mean that each person would have exactly the same measure. He came to give each of us eternal life and to reconcile every one of us to Himself. Now THAT is true fairness and no cause for jealousy.

October 20

"It will come about in all the land,"

Declares the Lord,

"That two parts in it will be cut off *and* perish;

But the third will be left in it.

"And I will bring the third part through the fire,

Refine them as silver is refined,

And test them as gold is tested.

They will call on My name,

And I will answer them;

I will say, 'They are My people,'

And they will say, 'The Lord is my God.'"

Zechariah 13:8-9

Tests come in many forms. Gold is tested with fire. While I'd prefer to avoid it, if it means being able to call on the Name of God and having Him refer to me as "My people," then absolutely! Refining it is, because you see, there is nothing better to be said than, "The Lord is my God."

October 21

Behold, the Lord has proclaimed to the end of the earth,

Say to the daughter of Zion,

"Lo, your salvation comes;

Behold His reward is with Him,

and His recompense before Him."

And they will call them, "The holy people,

The redeemed of the Lord";

And you will be called,

"Sought out, a city not forsaken."

Isaiah 62:11-12

I had to look up the word 'recompense' to make sure I understood it. It means, 'to make payment for services rendered.' Jesus Christ our salvation has come! He has brought eternal life and He brings our just rewards with Him! We ARE that holy people, the redeemed of the Lord and we most assuredly are those ones that are sought out, a city not forsaken! HALLELUJAH!

October 22

May He grant you your heart's desire

And fulfill all your counsel!

Psalm 20:4

This 'thought' seems to pop up about every six months in my daily 'thought.' Hmmm.

The literal word for 'counsel' here is 'purpose.'

Each of us has a reason for who we are, where we are, and when we are. When we give our lives to Him, He herds us down the path that leads where He would have us to go which of course, is to Him.

It seems to me that our heart's desire is His purpose. We almost always don't get there the way we had believed we would, but we DO get there and the end result is ever good!

October 23

This you know, my beloved brethren. But everyone must be quick to hear, slow to speak *and* slow to anger; for the anger of man does not achieve the righteousness of God.

James 1:19-20

For most of my life, I've held to the old saying; "Walk softly and carry a big stick." Not the most Godly of sayings to be sure.

I've seen firsthand what rage can do to a child and I include myself in this. Having no control over what's happening or not getting one's way is most often the cause of anger. Having the strength to not let it take control is a thing some never acquire. The thing is, uncontrolled anger and the righteousness of God have no place together. Displaying anger might give a momentary relief but it certainly doesn't achieve much else! To listen loudly, speak slowly and give one's anger to God, works. Letting Him carry it makes one's life, one's burdens ever so much easier to carry.

From now on, it's going to be; "Walk softly and let God." No stick required.

October 24

Only conduct yourselves in a manner worthy of the gospel of Christ, so that whether I come and see you or remain absent, I will hear of you that you are standing firm in one spirit, with one mind striving together for the faith of the gospel; in no way alarmed by *your* opponents—which is a sign of destruction for them, but of salvation for you, and that *too*, from God.

Philippians 1:27

What does one 'hear' of me. I wonder sometimes. Paul is pretty clear about what he expects of the Philippians. He wishes to hear of them "standing firm in one spirit, with one mind striving together for the faith of the gospel..." Pretty lofty expectations given the heart of man in general. His truly is an expectation of seeing fruit not of individuals but rather of each together with one mind, striving for the sake of the gospel. Let me suggest that he isn't looking for the First Baptist Church here nor Our Lady of Grace Catholic Church nor 'fill in the blanks' church. He is looking for a people whose individual walks are part of a body, no, THE BODY whose desire is to conduct themselves in a manner worthy of the gospel of Christ. Now THAT is a group I wish to be a part of and I'm pretty sure I can count you among its membership too.

October 25

He who walks in integrity walks securely,

But he who perverts his ways will be found out.

Proverbs 10:9

This is about staying on the path that leads to Him, always. It's about being in the light. It is good to have nothing to be 'found out' about.

October 26

A worthless man digs up evil, While his words are like scorching fire.

Proverbs 16:27

I know someone who is angry. The anger boils over in her demeanor, in her speech. She screams, demands, and hurts, not caring whether she leaves a burning path in her wake. While this verse is descriptive of her behavior let me make it clear that she like us all, is not beyond redemption. I was her. God in His mercy put out the flame of anger, of anguish which was me and in its place, gave me His words.

His words are filled with what is good, what builds up, and not that which tears down ....it's like a balm that clears the air of stink and I'm ever so grateful for it.

You know those words like a scorching fire? God burned them up too and ashes don't hurt, they nourish the soil.

October 27

Then he said to me, "This is the word of the Lord to Zerubbabel saying, 'Not by might nor by power, but by My Spirit,' says the Lord of hosts.

Zechariah 4:6

Well, I know each of you isn't Zerubbabel but the Word still stands. So often we (I specifically) try to 'push through' and to use everything within my power to get my way or to get something done. Not to say there isn't a place for that when one has a task that simply needs to get done. One needs to understand though, that it is His Spirit which does the accomplishing and it is us that He uses to do it. We're the water in the bucket and He does the pouring!

October 28

'Who is left among you who saw this temple in its former glory? And how do you see it now? Does it not seem to you like nothing in comparison? But now take courage, Zerubbabel,' declares the Lord, 'take courage also, Joshua son of Jehozadak, the high priest, and all you people of the land take courage,' declares the Lord, 'and work; for I am with you,' declares the Lord of hosts. 'As for the promise which I made you when you came out of Egypt, My Spirit is abiding in your midst; do not fear!' For thus says the Lord of hosts, 'Once more in a little while, I am going to shake the heavens and the earth, the sea also and the dry land. I will shake all the nations; and they will come with the wealth of all nations, and I will fill this house with glory,' says the Lord of hosts.

Haggai 2:3-7

May I suggest that Haggai prophetically spoke of the House of God in the latter days? His house IS being rebuilt and its cornerstone is Jesus Christ. This house IS filled with glory and we are to take courage! He is abiding in our midst and we are not to walk in fear while everything that can be shaken will be. In the midst of it, His is the wealth of the nations and it is ours to claim dear ones! It is ours!

October 29

As Jesus went on from there, He saw a man called Matthew, sitting in the tax collector's booth; and He said to him, "Follow Me!" And he got up and followed Him.

Matthew 9:9

I don't like to follow. It's that control thing again. I was recently in a store and found myself pushing a cart down the aisle with my husband in front of me on the side, holding onto the cart whilst steering it. My immediate reaction was to jerk it away from him, after all, who wants to be 'steered?' Then grace took a hold of me and I thought perhaps he was trying to help me push it. Still annoying but doable. Then I wondered if maybe the cart was helping HIM walk?

So often God wants to steer the cart and I pull away. At times He helps push it when I'm just too tired and care-worn. Then there are the times that He actually needs me to do the pushing, not because He is tired, but rather so that He can get me where I need to be to listen to Him. In those instances, I just need to know He's there. He didn't promise me a reason. He promised me eternal life!

My favorite times are when He tells me where He wants the cart to go beforehand. Just sayin.

October 30

When the devil had finished every temptation, he left Him until an opportune time. And Jesus returned to Galilee in the power of the Spirit, and news about Him spread through all the surrounding district.

Luke 4:13-14

Satan had thrown every temptation at Jesus with the result that "Jesus had returned to Galilee in the power of the Spirit."

I have been considering what 'an opportune time' in my own life looks like. We all have them. I for certain do and I usually can name them. Self-pity, unbelief, fear and I don't mean fear of God.

God's heart for us is to return "in the power of the Spirit." Not we but He.

October 31

Two things I asked of You,

Do not refuse me before I die:

Keep deception and lies far from me,

Give me neither poverty nor riches;

Feed me with the food that is my portion,

That I not be full and deny *You* and say,

"Who is the Lord?"

Or that I not be in want and steal,

And profane the name of my God.

Proverbs 30:7-9

When have I ever prayed: "Keep deception and lies far from me."?

Keep me from being 'full' (of myself) and help me remember from Whom I am fed.

When have I prayed: "Feed me with the food that is my portion."?

Perhaps it's time I started praying those words. Might be time for you too....

November

November 01

.......He Himself has said, "I will never desert you, nor will I ever forsake you," so that we confidently say,

"The Lord is my helper, I will not be afraid.

What will man do to me?"

Hebrews 13:5-6

I had a pretty good argument with my husband today. I felt that he was ignoring me and I wouldn't have it. A symptom of this is when he (or anyone else for that matter) walks away from an ongoing conversation or starts texting while the conversation is still going on. He had wanted to end our discussion because he'd tried to make a point about being responsible and I'd tried to explain why sometimes, not finishing a task wasn't always about being responsible! He'd said, "You always need to have your own opinion. Why can't you just agree with what I said?"

In a fit of anger (ten minutes later) I found him out in his workshop.

"I'm still mad at you! Do you know that most of my life has been spent trying to 'make peace'? I did it when I was growing up and I'm doing it now! ....and who says I need to agree with you anyway? Why isn't my opinion as important as yours?"

Why am I telling this tale? Because in the midst of the argument I realized that I no longer need to always try to be the 'helper' to smooth things over! I have THE HELPER to do it! My dear husband knew that exact moment too and gave me a hug and THAT is why God gave him to me!

November 02

When Elisha returned to Gilgal, *there was* a famine in the land. As the sons of the prophets were sitting before him, he said to his servant, "Put on the large pot and boil stew for the sons of the prophets." Then one went out into the field to gather herbs, and found a wild vine and gathered from it his lap full of wild gourds, and came and sliced them into the pot of stew, for they did not know *what they were*. So they poured *it* out for the men to eat. And as they were eating of the stew, they cried out and said, "O man of God, there is death in the pot." And they were unable to eat. But he said, "Now bring meal." He threw it into the pot and said, "Pour *it* out for the people that they may eat." Then there was no harm in the pot.

2 Kings 4:38-41

They had already eaten of the stew when the man of God threw the meal in. I too take poison in and believe me, there are many forms of poison. God though, is in the business of throwing meal into my pot. He turns what was meant for death, into life and it is life that is good and nourishing and gives me strength to go on. No death in the pot for me nor for you either!

318

November 03

Shout for joy, O heavens! And rejoice, O earth!

Break forth into joyful shouting, O mountains!

For the Lord has comforted His people

And will have compassion on His afflicted.

Isaiah 49:13

While reading Isaiah this morning I was struck with the thought that this Word was true then and is true now. Comfort for me takes on a bit of a different meaning than for most. When I'm wallowing in self-pity, He brings me up short and won't stand for it! He doesn't remind me of my shortcomings later either. In other words, He accepts me!

When I am truly 'afflicted' once again, there He is to bring help and relief and exactly what is needed. He has stood throughout the ages. Money in the bank so to speak; a Rock that I can stand on! He has compassion for His people and brings comfort, always, forever. Rejoice O earth!

November 04

Whatever house you enter, first say, 'Peace *be* to this house.' If a man of peace is there, your peace will rest on him; but if not, it will return to you.

Luke 10:5-6

My mom virtually always brought a small gift, a token along to those she visited. It might be a cake or a jar of jam but it was brought with a grateful heart. Peace is good to bring along as a gift, no matter where one visits. It is always readily at hand.

I've used this 'thought' just once, over all the years. I know it though. There are those dear ones whose house I visit where peace reigns. It settles on me when I walk in the door. It has nothing to do with the noise one hears or the clatter of busyness. It simply is where the peace of Jesus Christ rests. Those are the houses where I breathe a sigh of relief upon entering. It is good to have at one's own house too.

November 05

Open your mouth for the mute,

For the rights of all the unfortunate.

Open your mouth, judge righteously,

And defend the rights of the afflicted and needy.

Proverbs 31:8-9

Who gets to decide who the needy and the afflicted are? Exactly which ones are 'unfortunate?' It is relatively easy to decide when someone (whom you've already made your mind up about) has a connection to you. It gets more difficult when that someone is a stranger who has lashed out most likely because of some misery he or she is going through or it's someone who is living a less than exemplary lifestyle. What I read here is that there IS judgment. It is meant though, to be a righteous judgment coupled with a defense that stands in the gap. A place where one can be the bridge leading to God instead of the bridge leading to evil. A bridge is a good analogy for me personally because it carries with it the necessity of hanging in the air between two places, believing in faith that God Himself is truly at both ends.

November 06

"Either make the tree good and its fruit good, or make the tree bad and its fruit bad; for the tree is known by its fruit."

Matthew 12:33

I have a dear friend who said when faced with a difficult path ahead because of illness in the family which would run its course over a long length of time: "Every day is a good day."

I've often thought of that. You know, every day IS a good day. In the midst of pain and disappointment, being tired, and having to carry a huge load, every day IS a good day! The fruit that woman produces by her very presence is GOOD EVERY DAY! We are each known by our fruit.

November 07

The first to plead his case *seems* right,

Until another comes and examines him.

Proverbs 18:17

Ever listened to someone and you find yourself pretty well persuaded by their argument only to have your mind changed by someone else whose opinion differs from the first one you listened to? The keyword here seems to be 'examines.' Whose argument can stand up to scrutiny? There's a reason for sites like Snopes. If the world does it, may I suggest we should do the same? Our 'snopes' has a name too and it's called the 'Bible'. Happy examination!

November 08

All discipline for the moment seems not to be joyful, but sorrowful; yet to those who have been trained by it, afterwards it yields the peaceful fruit of righteousness. Therefore, strengthen the hands that are weak and the knees that are feeble, and make straight paths for your feet, so that *the limb* which is lame may not be put out of joint, but rather be healed.

Hebrews 12:11-13

Discipline comes in many forms. None seem to be particularly pleasant. There is such an exhilaration though, when I have stayed the course, allowed something to be corrected in my life, or pulled something through that has been particularly difficult. There is a stamina built which I can then draw on and I believe it is THAT which God is after in both you and me. The saying goes that 'misery loves company.' So does strength and more specifically when it comes from the hand of God.

November 09

"I will not leave you as orphans; I will come to you. After a little while the world will no longer see Me, but you *will* see Me; because I live, you will live also."

John 14:18-19

There are a lot of reasons why some are orphans. Abandonment, death, embarrassment, rejection to name a few. Jesus said He will not leave us as orphans. Because He lives, we live! What a word! Nothing the world can throw at us will ever have the power that this adoption in Him has!

This word means that I will never be adrift in a sea of doubt. I will never be plagued by thoughts of being alone or of being unwanted. HE has laid claim to me and it is forever folks. Same goes for you.

November 10

My eyes are continually toward the Lord,

For He will pluck my feet out of the net.

Psalm 25:15

Some nets are of my own making and some aren't. When my eyes are on the net, it's the only thing I can see. When they're on Him, I no longer particularly care if my feet are stuck or they aren't, because I know the Rock they're standing on, which is the very first step in His getting them unstuck.

November 11

....keep yourselves in the love of God, waiting anxiously for the mercy of our Lord Jesus Christ to eternal life.

Jude 21

For the past while as I've been praying, the thought often has come to me about 'keeping' in Christ Jesus. I must admit that at times it's a bit of a work. Hardness of heart creeps in, pushed along by the cares of the world, or by those things that cause me pain, admitted to or not. I must repeatedly make the choice to stay in His love. I must decide not to say "Oh my God" in a disrespectful manner. I must choose not to fill my mind with those things which are dribble or those things which God hates. I don't always make the correct choice but I'm always aware of which choice I've made. This truth is so basic and yet so essential to my life as I wait on Him. Pretty sure it's the same with you.

November 12

Those who sow in tears shall reap with joyful shouting.

He who goes to and fro weeping, carrying *his* bag of seed,

Shall indeed come again with a shout of joy, bringing his sheaves *with him*.

Psalm 126:5-6

What a wonderful Word. There is an end to tears and sorrow. There is an end to hopelessness and despair. It's the sowing. One has to experience carrying, the heaviness of the bag in the midst of stepping out of oneself to sow life. Ah but then, then comes the joy of bringing in the sheaves....and make no mistake, the end does come and it does bring joy!

November 13

Deliver those who are being taken away to death,

And those who are staggering to slaughter,

Oh hold *them* back.

If you say, "See, we did not know this,"

Does He not consider *it* who weighs the hearts?

And does He not know *it* who keeps your soul?

And will He not render to man according to his work?

Proverbs 24:11-12

This is about the dreaded word, 'responsibility.' Am I my brother's keeper? How about my neighbor or the guy who is like a scratchy fingernail on a blackboard to me when I even hear his voice? Besides, who am I to say a person is 'staggering to slaughter?' Sounds judgmental doesn't it? Well to an unbelieving world, yes it does. To those of us who know Him, it better sound like a charge to action.

We've been given a specific instruction here.

"Hold them back." and whilst doing it, understand that it is God who renders according to a person's work.

Cast aside excuses! Man up (or woman up for that matter)! Stand firm in the Body of Christ! Stand between 'them' and death! You can do it and so can I!

November 14

As the deer pants for the water brooks,

So my soul pants for You, O God.

Psalm 42:1

There is a song that sings it this way:

As the deer panteth for the water

So my soul longeth after Thee.

The world offers soda pop. It tastes great for a few seconds but try holding it in your mouth for any length of time.

There is a yearning though, a longing for a clear, cool drink of water. Its taste never grows stale. That is what He offers and the spring it flows from never runs dry. When one has tasted it, nothing else satisfies and that is as it should be.

November 15

"I will lead the blind by a way they do not know,

In paths they do not know I will guide them.

I will make darkness into light before them

And rugged places into plains.

These are the things I will do,

And I will not leave them undone."

Isaiah 42:16

A prophetic word here to the gentiles. A promise to the world of His faithfulness.

For me personally, it is a word well remembered. So often I can't see what is before me and so I try in my own strength to memorize the way so that I don't stumble or fall. God has given me a path to walk on and no, it isn't always familiar and it most probably isn't a way I would choose. Safety though is with God as my companion. It is He who guides me not by explaining what's on the path but rather by taking away the darkness because in Him there is no darkness. He says He will not leave these things undone and I believe Him. So should you.

November 16

When the whirlwind passes, the wicked is no more,

But the righteous *has* an everlasting foundation.

Proverbs 10:25

This 'thought' was posted a few days ago by a friend in MN (who incidentally isn't on this chain.) While I virtually always find the 'thought' by reading the Word, this one seemed to be what was right for today. There is a place which we stand on that the battering wind, the tornado, and the cares of the world cannot touch. It is the foundation, the Rock of our lives. I'm grateful that we share it.

Remember, a whirlwind clears the air and makes way for newness of life. The old is blown away but the Foundation stands.

November 17

The Lord is for me; I will not fear;

What can man do to me?

The Lord is for me among those who help me;

Therefore I will look *with satisfaction* on those who hate me.

Psalm 118:6-7

Well, there's quite a bit that man can do to me but you know, it isn't eternal. It isn't 'forever' and it isn't anything to fear because I have a hero who is for me. His Name is the Lord. He helps me and yes, He allows me, no strengthens me, to look upon those who hate me with a satisfied gleam in my eye. I'm pretty sure He has a sense of humor too.

November 18

It is good to give thanks to the Lord

And to sing praises to Your name, O Most High;

To declare Your lovingkindness in the morning

And Your faithfulness by night.

Psalm 92:1-2

I love these verses! My husband is a morning person. All is well in the morning. There is work to be done, people to see, letters to write. The doing brings a sense of accomplishment and for the most part all is well at the Schaefer ranch. Evenings are a different story. One can dwell on what hasn't been accomplished/completed, the disappointments heard about, etc. You get the picture. It is good that we pray together in the evenings because it sets us squarely in the position where we give thanks!

His faithfulness isn't always about finishing a task or being blessed unexpectedly. It's about an answer to a many-years-prayed-for situation, a life given to Christ, a loved one whose cancer is in remission.

Truth be told, His lovingkindness AND His faithfulness are ours both in the morning and by night. What a God we serve and have the privilege of calling on!

November 19

For the body is not one member, but many. But now God has placed the members, each one of them, in the body, just as He desired. And if one member suffers, all the members suffer with it; if *one* member is honored, all the members rejoice with it. Now you are Christ's body, and individually members of it.

1 Corinthians 12:14, 18, 26-27

I've used these Scriptures just this once and they are difficult for me. I admit it. They speak of taking up the burden, the suffering of others, of allowing a closeness which at times, I am ill-prepared for. The saying, "No pain, no gain." comes to mind. Truly though, this closeness also brings honor and celebration! Being a member of this club is open to any who wishes to join. The membership fee is our lives and the benefits are faith and hope and joy. I'm glad we're in it together.

November 20

"Blessed are those who hunger and thirst for righteousness, for they shall be satisfied."

Matthew 5:6

I recently had an encounter with someone who in our conversation, said that if she was to choose a 'religion' it would be buddhism. She went on to say that she believed in being good, being kind to others and taking care of the environment. I was flummoxed! I blurted out, "but that isn't enough! It isn't enough to be kind, to be good."

She had no sense of the reality of Jesus Christ. No hunger nor yearning for righteousness. Yes, I know....I'm around people all of the time who are the same way. I have to say though, that it was the first time that I felt truly without words! There wasn't anything to be said! She had made her decision.

She cannot have tasted the truth that to me is meat and drink. I live because He lives. I cannot be 'good' enough nor 'kind' enough to warrant eternal life and the forgiveness of my sins and neither can she! What I can do is pray that the Lord of the universe introduces Himself to her and that is exactly what I'm doing.

November 21

Let all bitterness and wrath and anger and clamor and slander be put away from you, along with all malice.

Ephesians 4:31

This is a verse that I've sought to live by for the past almost fifty years. It is a daily walk and I believe everyone who calls on the Name of Jesus has lived it too. It is for me at least, a continual decision to lay down bitterness, to not hold onto anger, and to put the clamor and slander of those things that would seek to catch me up...to set them aside. The choice is to be filled with God, to allow Him to blow the wind in my sails instead of those things that seek to halt me dead in my tracks. Sometimes the decision is easier than other times but it is always a good decision.....

November 22

Salt is good; but if the salt becomes unsalty, with what will you make it salty *again*? Have salt in yourselves, and be at peace with one another."

Mark 9:50

I just listened to a message by a fellow which led me to look up a few Scriptures pertaining to salt. I had never thought about salt as a preservative even though I've used it myself to make sauerkraut for example and of course salted salmon is one of my favorites.

We are to be the salt. We are to preserve those around us, encourage them to righteousness in their walk with God. Truly when the salt becomes unsalty when that zeal for the House of God has left one, what then is left? Salt doesn't burn. When fire is thrown upon it, the flame is much brighter but it doesn't burn. I love this metaphor. We are to be the salt of the earth, not burned by the fire of God but instead made brighter. Be salt dear ones, be salt.

November 23

Therefore they said to Him, "What shall we do, so that we may work the works of God?" Jesus answered and said to them, "This is the work of God, that you believe in Him whom He has sent."

John 6:28-29

I 'hope' I can believe enough; enough for what I 'want.' I 'hope' I will be able to 'perform' whatever it is that I wish to 'do' for God and His kingdom.

For me, hope is the engine and faith is the power. I can hope all I want but without power, it gets me nowhere. The power has never been what I could drum up. When I try, it gets me a few feet...but now faith, ah! It gets me to exactly where Jesus Christ is leading me. It's like adrenalin except that it never runs out.

Perhaps a better metaphor is that it is the blood in my veins. Always constant and ever on call. This faith, this lifeblood is this: "...that you believe in Him whom He has sent." Yep!

November 24

May my prayer be counted as incense before You;

The lifting up of my hands as the evening offering.

Psalm 141:2

Most often when I pray I'm asking for something...not usually for me, but for those the Holy Spirit puts on my heart to pray for. Sometimes though, I simply talk to God. Yes, it's prayer but it's not about asking. It's about listening and keeping close to Him and seeking to find what is on His heart.

We were just talking the other day about praying in the evening. In the morning there is hope for a good day, work to be done and positive things to look forward to. By evening at times hopes have been dashed, what one has wanted to accomplish hasn't gotten done and there often seems to be a kind of malaise that has set in. This 'thought' speaks to that. Let my disappointed prayer be counted as incense. Let the lifting of my hands truly be an evening offering when I'm tired and the lifting of my hands seems to be more difficult than it should be. Yes, in the evening, in the shadow of the day, oh God set a guard over my mouth and help me to keep a watch over the doors of my lips. I've said it before.... Morning prayers are hope. Evening prayers are faith!

November 25

But realize this, that in the last days difficult times will come. For men will be lovers of self, lovers of money, boastful, arrogant, revilers, disobedient to parents, ungrateful, unholy, holding to a form of godliness, although they have denied its power; Avoid such men as these.

2 Timothy 3:1-2, 5

The part I want to emphasize here is the last bit.

"...holding to a form of godliness, although they have denied its power; Avoid such men as these.

Here's the deal: If Satan can convince people that Godliness does not translate into drawing upon the power of God, to have it available and ready to help, then his battle has been won. I am here to tell you that it has not! Religion does not hold the power of God in its hands. Jesus Christ does.

November 26

There is a kind who is pure in his own eyes,

Yet is not washed from his filthiness.

Proverbs 30:12

This is a stern word. Many are the people who believe themselves 'good' enough, whether their hope is in doing good deeds or keeping the environment clean or serving the poor.....all worthy things to put one's hand to. They aren't good enough to clean the filthiness from one's soul though. Jesus Christ is the only one who can wash away the dirt and He offers to do it free of charge. For me at least, it is a continual sweeping of what has become unbelief and/or hurt and anger to make way for the simple honor of serving Him by what He puts before me. Pretty sure it's the same with you.

November 27

Let the redeemed of the Lord say *so*,

Whom He has redeemed from the hand of the adversary

And gathered from the lands,

From the east and from the west,

From the north and from the south.

He sent His word and healed them,

And delivered *them* from their destructions.

Psalm 107:2-3, 20

If I am guilty of anything, it is this. I do not make mention nearly enough of His having redeemed me from the hand of the adversary, of drawing me out of a world that was ugly and full of sin into a nation whose citizens are sons and daughters of the living God. His heart is to heal each one of us and deliver us from our destructions.

It is easy to hide one's faith under a bush or push it to the back of one's tongue when around unbelievers or for that matter, around those we love and cherish.

"I am redeemed!" I have been taken (in my case pushed) from the hand of the adversary into the land of the living. It is the same for you! He has gathered for Himself a people from every direction; a people whom He recognizes as His. Dare we not shout that very same recognition from the rooftops?

November 28

He also who is slack in his work

Is brother to him who destroys.

Proverbs 18:9

This is rather difficult for me to write about because it's rather touchy for me. I grew up in what could be described as a 'poor' house. In the midst of that, work was ever in the equation. There was no complaining either. I was very often moved from house to house and each time, in the midst of moving/working, my mom would set about cleaning, wallpapering, doing everything she could to make it a home, and let me tell you, some of those old farmhouses were difficult to make livable.

I've never seen a beggar's sign which says; "I need a job." It might make it a bit more amenable for me to help. Yes, on occasion I do help. It is as a result of the Holy Spirit giving me a nudge though. The lesson learned for me is that I find myself often saying to God; "I need a job." and you know, it's a pretty good thing to do. Suits me better than begging. Most likely you too.

November 29

For this reason I bow my knees before the Father, from whom every family in heaven and on earth derives its name, that He would grant you, according to the riches of His glory, to be strengthened with power through His Spirit in the inner man, so that Christ may dwell in your hearts through faith; *and* that you, being rooted and grounded in love, may be able to comprehend with all the saints what is the breadth and length and height and depth, and to know the love of Christ which surpasses knowledge, that you may be filled up to all the fullness of God.

Ephesians 3:14-19

Paul doesn't say here that he's praying for each of God's family members to get what they ask for. He's asking that God grant them via His Holy Spirit, the power in their inner man to live by faith, rooted there and grounded with love. It is a trusting that must come to everyone who in faith, believes that the circumstance they find themselves in, is allowed by God for a purpose. Does this mean that He allows difficult, awful things to happen? Well, it means that He uses every single circumstance to get each one where they need to go. It means that He turns ugliness into beauty. It means that by faith, each of us is to trust that He does know what He's doing. The end-all, of course, is that walking by faith allows a fullness in God which is obtained no other way and it is a good way!

November 30

One of His disciples, Andrew, Simon Peter's brother, said to Him, "There is a lad here who has five barley loaves and two fish, but what are these for so many people?" Jesus said, "Have the people sit down." Now there was much grass in the place. So the men sat down, in number about five thousand. Jesus then took the loaves, and having given thanks, He distributed to those who were seated; likewise also of the fish as much as they wanted.

John 6:8-11

Jesus told the disciples to have the people sit down before He fed them. Literally to recline, be inactive, idle. Five thousand people are quite a large number to tell to 'chill'. He could have fed them while they were standing. Sometimes I need to be fed. It might be food, it may be finances, it may be healing, and sometimes it may be something for someone else. You know where this is going. In the midst of my need, the best thing I can do is to be idle, to sit down and wait upon God who says He WILL distribute to those who are seated. Pretty sure it's the same for you. It's called faith and you know, we get as much as we want.

December

December 01

Be on your guard! If your brother sins, rebuke him; and if he repents, forgive him. And if he sins against you seven times a day, and returns to you seven times, saying, 'I repent,' forgive him."

Luke 17:3-4

I find myself sometimes wishing the person I'm angry with wouldn't ask for forgiveness. Then I would have an excuse to hold my anger close to me, if that makes sense. Note here that there is absolutely no justification given to cling to unforgiveness when forgiveness has been asked for, nor is there a limit to the number of days/times which one may ask to be forgiven. When I insist upon wearing this holding of a grudge like a coat of armor, it becomes a death shroud to me. Sober thought dear ones and yet, it is the essence of how Jesus is to us, limitless forgiveness!

December 02

Bear one another's burdens, and thereby fulfill the law of Christ.

Galatians 6:2

When I take on a load I place it across my back and am well able to bear the burden. Why do I mention this? Because there are ways for carrying and there is a time for allowing God to help carry. Whether the burden is upon one's back or heart or health, it is a part of life that God requires us to do. It is often painful in the short term but ah...in the long term, it brings joy to the heart and a light step and a strength to the body and to the soul.

To pick up someone else's load, one must often lay down one's own 'stuff' first. For me, that's been a critical thing to learn. So often (even when I'm complaining to God about having to do it) the doing of it opens my eyes to the realization that my own load really wasn't so very heavy after all and because God is who He is, He sends someone to help carry anyway.

December 03

The Lord is exalted, for He dwells on high;

He has filled Zion with justice and righteousness.

And He will be the stability of your times,

A wealth of salvation, wisdom and knowledge;

The fear of the Lord is his treasure.

Isaiah 33:5-6

The literal word for 'stability' is 'faithfulness.' There is this place that we stand on, which is the Rock of Jesus Christ. On that Rock are salvation, wisdom, knowledge, and faithfulness. In that place, justice and righteousness cover us and hide our nakedness.

I've given a lot of thought to "the fear of the Lord." There is salvation in that fear. If it was the only reason we have to follow Him, it is enough. Because of Who He Is though, there is so much more. There are wisdom and knowledge and justice and righteousness and yes, ever faithfulness. The fear of the Lord is generational too and each generation needs to come to its own understanding of what it means.

"Father, pour down upon us all of that fear which brings life to Your people and stability to Your Body!"

December 04

Guard, through the Holy Spirit who dwells in us, the treasure which has been entrusted to *you*.

2 Timothy 1:14

So often I've believed that I've used the deposit all up, spent it unwisely, or worse, I've cast it away as not being enough help. Yuck. One can believe the treasure doesn't exist or worse, use it for things that leave one empty. One can also spend it on what is good and has eternal value for His Kingdom's sake. I take it to heart that I must guard this treasure that is me, and in me, His Holy Spirit. So must you!

December 05

Rejoice in the Lord always; again I will say, rejoice!

Philippians 4:4

There have been a few times since I met Jesus when I've experienced a gut-wrenching sorrow. When the only escape has been sleep and it, fleeting. During those times, there has been this secret place, this flutter of life, this tiny flame that could not and would not be stomped out. It is the simple rejoicing in my soul that He is for me and not against me. He is ever-ready to help and His heart is always to seek my good. This jubilant Spirit has kept me, feeding my soul until I could again get my bearings. It is there for the taking and I take! So do you!

December 06

He said to the man with the withered hand, "Get up and come forward!" And He said to them, "Is it lawful to do good or to do harm on the Sabbath, to save a life or to kill?" But they kept silent. After looking around at them with anger, grieved at their hardness of heart, He said to the man, "Stretch out your hand." And he stretched it out, and his hand was restored.

Mark 3:3-5

Another name for hardness of heart is skepticism. Another one is jealousy and another unbelief. Each one of them carries an ugliness along with it. Jesus was angry and got beyond it, past it if you will. It became grief and then compassion. It is no easy task to go from anger to healing in an instant but it is truly a model we are to follow as we are to follow the Modeler.

December 07

Pure and undefiled religion in the sight of *our* God and Father is this: to visit orphans and widows in their distress, *and* to keep oneself unstained by the world.

James 1:27

Unblemished, untainted, clean, unsullied....all words to describe keeping oneself 'unstained' by the world. I remember my baptism forty-plus years ago in Prairie Lake, Grand Rapids, MN like it was yesterday. The realization of truly what it meant came a few months later. I was sitting on a stool at a print shop (same location as our church) when an acid flashback hit me. I'd never had one before and it took me by surprise! Almost instantly though, I made a declaration out loud that; "All of this has been washed away by the Blood of the Lamb and I am clean! I rebuke you satan!" Let me tell you, instantly whatever it was, flew away, never to return again. I've occasionally thought about that experience as the years have gone by and have applied it to those deceptions which seek to sidetrack me.

I have certainly visited widows and worked with 'orphans.' The keeping oneself unstained has been a bit more work but the end result was then and is now...that yes, I am 'religious' and I am unstained because the Lord of all the earth keeps me washed clean. Same goes for you.

354

December 08

Evening and morning and at noon,

I will complain and murmur,

And He will hear my voice.

Psalm 55:17

One of the grandsons gets frustrated at times because no one is listening to him (from his perspective). He isn't being heard. Whether he's correct in his verbal complaint (screaming) or not makes no difference. He just desires to be heard, to have someone respond to his little heart.

Evening and morning and in the middle of the day pretty much mean the entire day. He hears my voice always, every time I speak to Him. It doesn't matter whether I complain, murmur, scream or pray. He hears, and His heart is to answer every single time.

December 09

O Lord, I beseech You, may Your ear be attentive to the prayer of Your servant and the prayer of Your servants who delight to revere Your name, and make Your servant successful today and grant him compassion before this man."

Now I was the cupbearer to the king.

Nehemiah 1:11

The last sentence of this verse; "Now I was cupbearer to the king." has many times touched my own heart. God placed Nehemiah exactly where he needed to be, when he needed to be there to do God's bidding. How often He does that. Nehemiah didn't question why he'd been given the job he held as cupbearer. He was there to get the king's ear and to do what needed to be done and he did it because He revered God and asked not for himself, but rather to be shown favor and compassion to enable him to complete the task. How often in my own life I've been given a task. I'd like to tell you that I've always been that one who doesn't question, why me and made the focus about Him instead of me but neither would be true.

I might not be 'cupbearer to the king' but I should be ever ready to do what I've been placed by God to do. Each of us is a 'cupbearer.'

December 10

Then behold, a hand touched me and set me trembling on my hands and knees. He said to me, "O Daniel, man of high esteem, understand the words that I am about to tell you and stand upright, for I have now been sent to you." And when he had spoken this word to me, I stood up trembling. Then he said to me, "Do not be afraid, Daniel, for from the first day that you set your heart on understanding *this* and on humbling yourself before your God, your words were heard, and I have come in response to your words.

Daniel 10:10-12

Let our battle cry be that of Daniel who set his heart on discerning what God was after, on humbling himself before Him. God's response to him was that he was a man beloved, esteemed by God.

Our God is the same God who heard Daniel. His response today is the same as it was to him; to send help when we seek it, when we humble ourselves before Him. We pursue, He comes.

December 11

Sow with a view to righteousness,

Reap in accordance with kindness;

Break up your fallow ground,

For it is time to seek the Lord

Until He comes to rain righteousness on you.

Hosea 10:12

This Scripture was actually spoken to rebellious Israel. They had been given much and esteemed it little.

This is a word for today, for every day! It is a call to sow what is good. The guarantee here is that then, oh then....kindness springs up to be reaped.

Each of us must break up those empty parts of our heart which sit unused and perhaps unrecognized. Seek the Lord today and every day until He comes; until He reigns down righteousness!

Hallelujah!

December 12

For many deceivers have gone out into the world, those who do not acknowledge Jesus Christ *as* coming in the flesh. This is the deceiver and the antichrist.

2 John 7

Since I came to know Jesus, belief in Him has been a slam dunk for me. I believe it's because I couldn't imagine going back to my old life without Him. Such a daily, hopeless drudge. There is for sure a deceiver though. It is the hopelessness of the world all rolled into unbelief. I'm forever grateful that I have broken through that world; that sham of a life to see and be a part of what is real and true; looking at the world through the lens of Jesus Christ.

December 13

Grace be with all those who love our Lord Jesus Christ with incorruptible *love*.

Ephesians 6:24

Grace is defined as "A manifestation of favor."

When I pray for our family, very often I pray favor down upon their heads. When I send birthday greetings I pray the favor of God upon the one who has a birthday. I am in good company. Paul set a wonderful example!

May grace, yes favor, be upon you, each of you who love our Lord Jesus Christ with incorruptible love!

AMEN!

December 14

And a man who had been lame from his mother's womb was being carried along, whom they used to set down every day at the gate of the temple which is called Beautiful, in order to beg alms of those who were entering the temple. When he saw Peter and John about to go into the temple, he *began* asking to receive alms. But Peter, along with John, fixed his gaze on him and said, "Look at us!" And he *began* to give them his attention, expecting to receive something from them. But Peter said, "I do not possess silver and gold, but what I do have I give to you: In the name of Jesus Christ the Nazarene—walk!" And seizing him by the right hand, he raised him up; and immediately his feet and his ankles were strengthened.

And on the basis of faith in His name, *it is* the name of Jesus which has strengthened this man whom you see and know; and the faith which *comes* through Him has given him this perfect health in the presence of you all.

Acts 3:2-7, 16

The man asked for alms, not healing. The faith which he had upon hearing the Name of Jesus, strengthened him; healed him. If you think about it, he really had no other choice. Peter pulled him up! We have that same Name on our lips and the same power to speak!

December 15

Do you not know that those who run in a race all run, but *only* one receives the prize? Run in such a way that you may win.

1 Corinthians 9:24

This takes dogged determination. The kind where one gets bone-weary and keeps going....knowing that the end WILL come, and when it does, there is a prize awaiting the winner that is beyond value. It is a race that Jesus Christ ran and won and He bountifully shares the win with all. If I have a hope, and I do....it is that we accept those winnings, that prize with graciousness and perseverance and strength. Oh, and loyalty too because it's important.

December 16

Let your eyes look directly ahead

And let your gaze be fixed straight in front of you.

Proverbs 4:25

Jesus Christ is straight ahead. One doesn't need to squint to see Him either.

December 17

If Christ is in you, though the body is dead because of sin, yet the spirit is alive because of righteousness. But if the Spirit of Him who raised Jesus from the dead dwells in you, He who raised Christ Jesus from the dead will also give life to your mortal bodies through His Spirit who dwells in you.

Romans 8:10-11

I've had to give this Scripture a bit of a think. My spirit is alive in Christ Jesus. According to this, so is my body. That doesn't mean I won't die. It means that while my body has breath, I am continually experiencing LIFE quite literally in my mortal body by the very same Spirit which raised Christ from death! I do not have a 'sinned' body, I have a 'saved' body. Wonder-working power my dears; wonder-working power!

December 18

But all things become visible when they are exposed by the light, for everything that becomes visible is light.

Ephesians 5:13

No more hiding! When sin is found out, it becomes light! No more guilt, no more shame, no more carrying a load which man is not meant to bear! When ALL THINGS are exposed to light, everything becomes LIGHT! AMEN and Hallelujah! God intended to lead every one of us to the light, not to shame us but rather to enable us to give the load to Him. To bring relief to His people! He IS the Light!

December 19

A tranquil heart is life to the body,

But passion is rottenness to the bones.

Proverbs 14:30

I've wanted something so badly that it made me sick, quite literally. It is not something I speak proudly of. Passion here isn't speaking of a sexual desire. It is rather speaking of an excessive demanding or obsession for something. That wanting does indeed, make the bones rotten. It is seeking after a thing in spite of God instead of because of God.

Tranquility, on the other hand, is when I am able to be even-keeled. It is being free from those emotional roller-coasters which keep me unsteady at best and constantly fearful at worst. A tranquil heart is absolutely life to my body! Yours too!

December 20

His master said to him, 'Well done, good and faithful slave. You were faithful with a few things, I will put you in charge of many things; enter into the joy of your master.'

Matthew 25:21

You know the story of the talents. Jesus didn't tell the man given one talent or the man given two talents to demand social justice nor equal pay, same as the man given five talents. He told each of them to do well with what he was given. That's us, folks. We're to use what we're given and invest it into the Kingdom of God and the result; Oh the wonder of it! We get to enter into the joy of our master!

December 21

"It will come about at that time

That I will search Jerusalem with lamps,

And I will punish the men

Who are stagnant in spirit,

Who say in their hearts,

'The Lord will not do good or evil!'

Zephaniah 1:12

'Stale' and 'foul from standing' are definitions of 'stagnant.' It doesn't paint a pretty picture. My dad used to say, "You'd have to drive a stake to see if he's moving." when he was describing someone he considered lazy. It is one thing to stand still when considering how one is to move forward. It is another thing entirely to do it when one is simply lazy or 'lazy in spirit.'

Whether it's Jerusalem or New York City or Kalamazoo, He still is searching with lamps to root out those ones who say in their heart "The Lord will not do good or evil!" May God keep me from this dull-willed, spiritual sluggishness. You too!

December 22

The Lord is the one who goes ahead of you; He will be with you. He will not fail you or forsake you. Do not fear or be dismayed."

Deuteronomy 31:8

Job says;

"But as for me, I would seek God,

And I would place my cause before God;

"So the helpless has hope...."

Moses declares who/what that hope is....It is He who goes ahead of us; who is with us, who does not fail nor forsake us.

There is an end to suffering, an end to pain. God does not say we won't be required to walk its path. He says that He will be there with us, to lend us strength when we stumble and to carry us when we cannot walk. It is not an easy thing to ask for that kind of help. When we do, it is reckoned to us as righteousness.

December 23

Now may the God of peace Himself sanctify you entirely; and may your spirit and soul and body be preserved complete, without blame at the coming of our Lord Jesus Christ. Faithful is He who calls you, and He also will bring it to pass.

1 Thessalonians 5:23-24

Laying down a grudge is hard for me. I admit it. I like to hold onto it, massage it and justify its existence. Especially if the holding of it pertains to someone who I've perceived as making fun of me or of those I love. Pretty shallow huh?

I have a pattern to go by though which shows a different diagram. It displays a 'complete' picture of me without blame, with a sanctity of Spirit which has the promise included with it that YES, in fact, it is how Jesus Christ sees me! He's called me you see, and in the calling, He's said He'll bring it to pass. You've received that same calling. Glad we're mates. The 'grudge' load was too heavy to carry anyway.

December 24

Then Jesus again spoke to them, saying, "I am the Light of the world; he who follows Me will not walk in the darkness, but will have the Light of life."

John 8:12

Since I've gotten saved, I haven't cared much for the darkness. I'm not afraid of it, I just don't like it. One stumbles around, not sure of the direction...settling for the big picture because one can't see the small things, the details. Let me say again; I don't like it. I see clearly now. I need not depend upon myself to provide the light. I have it and will have it for eternity. So will you. I like that!

December 25

Answer a fool as his folly *deserves*,

That he not be wise in his own eyes.

Proverbs 26:5

I'm still learning about this one. Sometimes it isn't for me so much about what "his folly deserves," as it is about what I believe he deserves. My go-to is to let the sucker have it, whether his folly deserves it or not. That doesn't help him though. If anything it locks him into a box of my making which he can't fight his way out of without defending the mistake. Then who's the fool? There is a reason Jesus spoke in His own defense by using parables and asking questions. They are a light in the darkness and exactly do what this Scripture says. They point out the foolishness to those who reject the truth while at the same time, making room for the light to shine through the darkness.

December 26

Let Your lovingkindness, O Lord, be upon us,

According as we have hoped in You.

Psalm 33:22

I have had many hopes in my life. I've hoped for 'stuff' and a beautiful location to hang my hat. I have hoped that my children each love and serve God all of their days (that one goes without saying, I've prayed, declared, and hoped it so much). I've hoped for finances when the need has come up and I've hoped for Jesus Christ to come back. I have to admit that I haven't always been in a hurry for that last one because you know, I love life quite a bit the way it is. With all of these hopes, life seems to always come back to that which unites us into just one hope, one faith, and one Body.

He IS our hope.

December 27

"Many waters cannot quench love, Nor will rivers overflow it; If a man were to give all the riches of his house for love, It would be utterly despised."

Song of Solomon 8:7

I was lying in bed last evening in the middle of the night. I had been awakened by my husband getting up and couldn't go back to sleep. My thoughts strayed to this guy, the one whose fault it was that I was wide awake and you know, I realized I just love him! I have been annoyed at him but not dismayed. I have been angry but not to the point of disgust. I simply cherish him and am ever so grateful for him. The love that I have for him has been a good pattern for me. It has steadied my path and yes, it is surely priceless.

The best part is, he loves both God and me. So does God; love me that is.

December 28

Let your light shine before men in such a way that they may see your good works, and glorify your Father who is in heaven.

Matthew 5:16

There are so many things I could say about what I've received from reading the Scriptures in order to put these 'thoughts' into words. If there has been any work done, any glory to be given, let it be to the One who in return has given me life and oh, what a life it has been.

From its inception, this 'thought' has been about honoring God, His Son, and the Holy Spirit. It's been about sharing what He's done and meant to me. I say again, they are His 'thoughts' and His glory. I have always and continue to hold fast to the fact that Scripture does not return empty. It sinks into one's very soul, becoming a part of who each of us is. Thanks ever so much for reading.

December 29

Then Jonah prayed to the Lord his God from the stomach of the fish, and he said,

"I called out of my distress to the Lord,
And He answered me.
I cried for help from the depth of Sheol;
You heard my voice.
"Those who regard vain idols
Forsake their faithfulness,
But I will sacrifice to You
With the voice of thanksgiving.
That which I have vowed I will pay.
Salvation is from the Lord."

Jonah 2:1-2, 8-9

I haven't cried from the belly of a whale. I HAVE cried from bellies of my own making. They have been just as deep and just as filled with death.

Jonah's response to God is to shout with grateful praise.

"SALVATION COMES FROM THE LORD!"

It was true then and it is true now and I am ever so grateful. Let me add my own to those shouts!

"SALVATION COMES FROM THE LORD!"

December 30

Then Mordecai told *them* to reply to Esther, "Do not imagine that you in the king's palace can escape any more than all the Jews. For if you remain silent at this time, relief and deliverance will arise for the Jews from another place and you and your father's house will perish. And who knows whether you have not attained royalty for such a time as this?"

Esther 4:13-14

I have often considered this Scripture. I haven't been placed in a king's palace but I most assuredly have been placed in a situation that I knew was a 'for such a time as this' situation. God will get done what needs to be done with or without me. Being in my personal comfort zone isn't what's required. It's the knowing that God will give me the strength and ability to do what He's put before me to do and His will is infinitely more important than mine. May I ever have the spiritual ears to hear when He calls; "For such a time as this."

You too.

December 31

Now to Him who is able to do far more abundantly beyond all that we ask or think, according to the power that works within us, to Him *be* the glory in the church and in Christ Jesus to all generations forever and ever. Amen.

Ephesians 3:20-21

Weariness comes from carrying a load we weren't meant to carry. The power within us can be used to carry bricks of anger, of resentment, of worry, of pain, and of unforgiveness....and pretty soon, the very promises that God has for us are seemingly unobtainable. HE SAYS He is ABLE to do FAR MORE ABUNDANTLY beyond ALL that we ask or think, according to the POWER that WORKS WITHIN US! My hope for you is this; that you give HIM the bricks to carry and that each of you allows HIM to use that POWER He's put within you to do more than you could ask for or hope for or imagine for!

you don't control the wind
but you can adjust the sails.